THE END

THE END

NARRATION
AND CLOSURE
IN THE CINEMA

RICHARD NEUPERT

 WAYNE STATE UNIVERSITY PRESS   DETROIT

Library of Congress Cataloging-in-Publication Data
Neupert, Richard John.
    The end : narration and closure in the cinema / Richard Neupert.
    p. cm. — (Contemporary film and television series)
    Includes bibliographical references and index.
    ISBN 0-8143-2525-4 (pbk. : alk. paper)
    1. Motion pictures. 2. Closure (Rhetoric) I. Title.
II. Series.
PN1995.N388 1995
791.43—dc20   94-38732

Designer: Joanne Elkin Kinney

For Caroline, Cathy,
and
Sophie

CONTENTS

ACKNOWLEDGMENTS

I am pleased to be able to thank and acknowledge many of the people who aided me throughout the research and writing of this study. I received generous grants at various stages of research, including a Travel Grant to Paris from the University of Wisconsin Graduate School and another from the University of Wisconsin's Department of Communication Arts. I was also fortunate enough to benefit from my wife Catherine Jones's fellowship to the École des Chartres in Paris which provided time and research opportunities that helped me complete the initial manuscript. At Georgia Institute of Technology, the Literature, Communication, and Culture Department, and in particular Ken Knoespel and Ione Sibley have been essential in providing support, photographic equipment, and access to films.

Individuals who provided beneficial criticisms, film suggestions, and strong encouragement from the earliest stages include Eric Smoodin, Leslie Midkiff-DeBauche, Kevin Hagopian, Laura Thielen, and especially Matthew Bernstein and Jim Peterson. I also wish to thank Vance Kepley, J. J. Murphy, Peter Schofer, Sidney Levy, Kristin Thompson, Jacques Aumont, and Marc Vernet for their very productive and challenging input; they helped shape this project. David Bordwell's guidance, energy, and professional rigor were and are instrumental to my work. There is no better teacher.

The director at Wayne State University Press, Arthur B. Evans, has provided valuable assistance and much appreciated persistence throughout the publication process, and suggestions from Editor Lynn H. Trease and Series Editor Patricia Erens have been very useful. I also want to thank my family: my mother Caroline Neupert has provided unfailing support and my brothers Mike and Jim have been incredibly generous. Finally, I offer my deepest gratitude and devotion to Cathy Jones; her understanding, intellect, and spirit inspire and guide everything I do.

9

CHAPTER 1

INTRODUCTION

A narrative has *a beginning and an ending*, a fact that
simultaneously distinguishes it from the rest of the world.
—Christian Metz[1]

Endings and Narration

As anyone who has ever peeked at the last page of a novel before
actually "getting there" knows, guessing where a story is heading is
one of the key pleasures and anxieties of reading. During the first third
of a movie at our local movie theater, of course, we cannot dash back
to the projection booth to ask to glimpse the last few minutes of a
thriller, but the desire to anticipate just where the story is going shapes
our every moment in front of a motion picture. Regardless of our
ability to know the ending ahead of time, we also have to admit that in
certain genres and modes of production the "value" of knowing the
eventual resolution varies dramatically. It does not take a Ph.D. in Film
Studies, for instance, to guess that Lucy Warriner in *The Awful Truth*
(McCarey, 1937) will end up back with her nearly ex-husband Jerry
rather than Dan Leeson; after all, in addition to all the textual clues and
generic rules, Jerry is played by Cary Grant and Leeson by perennial
"loser" Ralph Bellamy (see fig. 1.1). But watching the inevitable fall
into place is part of the genre film pleasure. However, it would be
nearly impossible to guess that N will die in a car crash in *L'Immortelle*
(Robbe-Grillet, 1963), that Antoine Doinel will eventually run to the

Fig. 1.1. *The Awful Truth.* Happy Ending:
Jerry and Lucy Warriner reunited

ocean in *The 400 Blows* (Truffaut, 1959), or that Corinne in *Weekend* (Godard, 1967) will become a leftist cannibal. Moreover, simply knowing these art film endings does not seem to provide us the same sort of satisfaction or significance as in cause-effect ordered genre films. The goal of *The End* is precisely to come to terms with how different films, working within diverse eras and traditions, follow very different paths for how they tell their stories, but also for when and how they decide to *stop* telling their stories.

Literary and film critics have always been concerned with determining the principles of narrative construction or organization. Narratology by definition is dedicated to studying textual structures and logic in order to understand better how narratives tell their stories, how one text's production process differs from that of another, and how textual strategies manipulate the audience's labor and rewards. In film studies, film *beginnings* have long been recognized as a privileged part of the narrative, since they consciously and directly address the spectator—the opening credits roll and the first scenes begin to integrate the audience into a particular viewing experience.[2] Yet while the importance of *endings* has always been evident, no rigorous studies have been undertaken to investigate their specific functions and how they inform cinematic narration.

The most exemplary studies on literary endings are Frank Kermode's *The Sense of an Ending*, Barbara Herrnstein Smith's *Poetic Closure*, and David Richter's *Fable's End*. There are certainly many other helpful book-length studies of literary endings, including John Gerlach's *Toward the End*, an investigation of structure in the American short story, Elizabeth MacArthur's *Extravagant Narratives* on epistolary novels, Armine Kotin Mortimer's *La Clôture narrative*, Marianna Torgovnick's *Closure in the Novel*, and Rachel Blau DuPlessis's analysis of women writers, *Writing Beyond the Ending*. The analyses by Smith and Richter go beyond most literary work on endings, however, and serve as fertile ground for testing where literary criticism excels and where it falls short of accomplishing a detailed study of endings. Both Smith and Richter approach their respective objects of study by opposing strong methods of closure with weak ones. They assert that strong, secure closure involves the achievement first, of a definite sense of completeness, and second, a structurally determined stylistic closure.

Smith's goal is to determine why one point is more appropriate than another for ending a poem. She distinguishes between "endings" and "conclusions," writing that any event, narrative or otherwise, may simply stop or end; only a text or art work may *conclude*, with the conclusion coming at a definite "termination point."[3] She writes that "Closure may be regarded as a modification of structure that makes *stasis*, or the absence of further continuation, the most probable succeeding event."[4] Thus, for Smith, endings are judged by their appropriateness to overall structure and the narrated events or context, but she could go even further in tying her evaluation of endings to how readers read.

In *Fable's End*, Richter helpfully differentiates "thematic completeness" (character goals are achieved and all major events have been played out), from "stylistic closure": "In fables . . . the aesthetic pleasure of endings is at least as much due to achieved completeness as to good closure devices."[5] According to Richter, a narrative can complete its story action but still have weak or inappropriate "devices" for ending the work. He also asserts that in less conventional fables the central plot is left "more or less up in the air" at the end; thus themes may be left incomplete, failing to answer whether the protagonist obtained his/her major goal, but overall stylistic closure can still remain intact.[6] Like Smith, Richter's model of a dual narrative structure assumes two aspects to a narrative, one involving story and theme, the other employing style and narration.

13

These literary models, do help outline what a useful account of narration and endings must accomplish. They suggest that ending a text involves two interdependent levels or textual operations, one involving the story and one involving narration. Other critics, such as Julia Kristeva, also separate and evaluate story resolution and the degree of closure provided by the narration.[7] My study continues these traditions yet adapts the duality of narrative completion to cinematic texts by building the variety, function, and effect of various strategies of closure into a comprehensive narrative model. Thus, *The End* clarifies terms and methods for analyzing just how filmic narratives end and how the progression toward those ends guides the viewer's complex activities of perception, comprehension, and expectation.

Toward a Semiotics of Narrative Closure

In *The Open Work*, Umberto Eco analyzes narrative closure but expresses reservations about just how meaningful his categories "open" and "closed" can ever be: "Openness, in the sense of a fundamental ambiguity in the message, is a constant of art works, and we cannot clearly see how meaningful the expression 'a closed work' could be."[8] Eco goes on to explain that his concept " 'open work' is not a critical category, but a *hypothetical model*," which will allow critics to begin making a sketch of one tendency in contemporary art.[9] The degree of openness in an art work, for Eco, can never be absolute, and the terms "closed" and "open" remain metaphors for structural characteristics rather than concrete operations.

In contrast to Eco, my desire is indeed to break films into "critical categories," since by constantly discussing the strategies of openness and closure in relation to some vague sliding scale between absolute openness and perfect closure, we actually fail to address closure. Eco's model sidesteps the specific goal of testing how texts end by looking only for the ways they differ from other extreme examples. Ending a text, like beginning one, is an essential part of constructing a narrative. For both the individual spectator and the film critic, therefore, the interpretation of a text's conclusion must relate to the interpretation of the text as a whole. As Marc Vernet writes, "This enclosure of the narrative is important to the extent that, on the one hand, it acts as an organizing element of the text that is conceived as a function of its finality; on the other hand, it allows the elaboration of the textual system(s) that make up the narrative."[10]

The sort of narrative model needed to account for complex narration and its endings must adequately contain what other critics have termed "theme," "form," "story," and "style." Semiology is quite capable of making these functions clearer and more defined and it also allows us to isolate the activity of the spectator in relation to production of a "telling" and a "told" in the narrative. Neither process can exist or operate independently of the other, since "what is told" needs the narrating process to exist. Thus a narrative consists of two processes just as a sign is composed of the interdependent signifier and signified.

From the beginning, semiotics has had as its goal what Ferdinand de Saussure outlined as a "science for the study of the life of signs at the center of social life."[11] As Roland Barthes explains in the preface to *Communications* 4, "semiology took as its object of study all sign systems, whatever their material form, whatever their limitations: images, gestures, melodic sounds, the objects and drives involved in ritual . . . and if these are not always 'languages,' at least they are signifying systems."[12] Thus, while semiotics began by keeping very close to linguistic analysis, its overall project has always been to pull in any social science methodology that informs the production and comprehension of signs, codes, and finally significance.

One of the chief problems of semiotic analysis, however, has been the ambiguity and even contradiction in its terminology, especially evident in film studies' adaptation and reworking of the terms enunciation and enounced (*énonciation/énoncé*) and Emile Benveniste's linguistic pairing of *histoire* and *discours*.[13] The problem with using terms like histoire and discours, is that they have been adapted by many different critics, so their meaning changes between Benveniste, Barthes, Metz, and Gérard Genette. In selecting a vocabulary and narrative model we should understand the history of such semio-linguistic terms. This study, however, will retain the more functional labels *story* and *narrative discourse*. I accept the theorization of "narrative" as a double process: First, as the story, or represented level; and second, as the narrative discourse, or representational level. This approach treats any text as a dynamic relation between narrative discourse and story, so that we might understand narration, and more specifically endings, as the results of a productive process between these two signifying systems. An ending involves both story resolution and closure of the narrative discourse, necessitating a clear definition of both story and discursive functions. This binary narrative model allows us to separate more

15

clearly what Richter and Smith call "completeness of theme" from "closure devices."

Story and Resolution

In defining a story, we face the necessary but seemingly impossible task of devising an essential and complete account of what a minimal story actually is. For Christian Metz, the filmic story is "a temporal sequence of events";[14] story is here required to contain more than one event and inscribe some fictional time scheme. Jonathan Culler also describes the story as a "reported sequence of events."[15] One problem is that these definitions are so broad that more kinds of texts than strictly narrative ones could be included, since any text that can be interpreted as a sequencing of events might be defined as having a story. The definition needs something more. Tzvetan Todorov's explanation that a story has two levels—the logic of events and characters—begins to make story more precise.[16] Seymour Chatman defines story by referring to Louis Hjelmslev's semiotic grid: story is the *content* of the film's narrative expression, and is also a continuum, or the total set of all conceivable events.[17] Chatman thereby builds in the notion of diegesis, allowing for the fact that no series of events can be completely shown in a text—narrative ordering necessarily involves reduction and ellipsis on the story level.

These definitions all bring up the question of where the story actually is for the spectator. If a story can include events not fully shown, as Culler asserts, then not all story elements need to be seen or heard. Story, according to Todorov, remains abstract; it is perceived and reconstructed by the spectator while it is performed by the narrative discourse. Stories are composed of events, which Chatman defines clearly as "either *actions (acts)* or *happenings*. Both are changes of state."[18] By labelling an action as a change of state, Chatman allows for temporal ordering or progression and can equate his definition with the Formalists' concept of a motif. An "action" involves a character as its agent, while a "happening" uses a character or other story existent as its object. Thus, story events exist within story time, while story existents inhabit story space.[19] Characters, their actions, and surrounding existents (elements of setting) all make up story, and give it spatial and temporal dimensions.

So far, then, the story is a series of events containing characters, actions, and settings. The degree of causality between the actions will be one of the variables in the films discussed in this study, while the type of cause-effect logic that underlies the action strongly influences the degree of story resolution. Since every story event is not equally critical to the progression from one act or state to another, and given that all characters will not be equally central in the determination of various story events, we need to distinguish between primary and secondary story components. Barthes defines such components as functions and indices: cardinal functions are those with primary or "hinge" functions, while catalyzers are more complementary or secondary. A cardinal function opens or closes an alternative path; therefore, these functions are more "consequential" than catalyzers.[20] Indices may be divided as well into *indices* proper, and *informants*. Indices signify a feeling, atmosphere, or even psychological state (Barthes uses "suspicion" as an example), while informants "always serve to authenticate the reality of the referent," by helping embed the fiction into a diegetic world. The way *Weekend*'s Roland shifts his car hurriedly would be an index of his impatience, while the mileage and hour intertitles are informants of his progress.

In semiotics, signs may be linked together into formal models or codes to become significant in relation to other signs and to embody a larger signifying system. The isolation of narrative codes is one viewing activity and entails locating, following, and understanding various narrative units specific to every text. A story is thus a complex system of characters, actions, and events, organized temporally and possibly according to causality, and all reconstructed by the viewer's activity, but the codes for narrative progression and completion must be further explained. For instance, while the basic story could simply involve our perception of events, we must also allow for the text's varying degree of completion of story codes. Here Todorov is again quite helpful in defining the basic complete narrative: "An 'ideal' narrative begins with a stable situation which is disturbed by some power or force. There results a state of disequilibrium; when a force is directed in the opposite direction, the equilibrium is re-established."[21] While this account sounds more like a physics experiment than a summary of narrative, it does outline the one element necessary for the perception of a complete or resolved story: the achievement of some equilibrium, or stasis point.

A story is logically divided into actions, characters, and existents which may also be defined as functions and indices. A complete action, therefore, would be one that moves from a cardinal story node to some resolution of that story function. For example, a large story action may be that the sheriff must keep a murderer locked in jail until the judge arrives in town to hold a trial. This sort of action already has its own inscribed termination point since it implies that the sheriff will either succeed or fail. Either way, the hermeneutic of "Will the sheriff be capable of holding the prisoner?" would have to be answered for the action to be perceived as resolved. In *Rio Bravo* (Hawks, 1959) this single action takes several hours of screen time before it can be completed.

A film, however, is rarely composed of one single action code. The simple definition of a story event allows for such things as "riding into town," "the sun sets," or "the sheriff plays poker with the prisoner," to constitute events in a Western. Thus, whether an event has a cardinal or catalyzing function, it may be interpreted in terms of whether or not it is accomplished. A duel to the death in a Western will obviously have a more conclusive result than an event like "the sheriff walks his rounds," yet both events require an ending, even if it is only inferred by the spectator or referred to by other characters. Quite often the resolution of events in classical Hollywood films is parodied, as in *Support Your Local Sheriff* (Kennedy, 1969), in which James Garner's character claims he is "just passing through on his way to Australia." Unlike the classic westerner, however, he never does leave.

Story resolution demands the termination of the large action codes that propel and dominate the narrative events and characters. In a melodrama like *All that Heaven Allows* (Sirk, 1955), the story's resolution involves the final decision by Cary (Jane Wyman) whether to follow her heart and stay with gardener Ron Kirby (Rock Hudson); this decision marks the culmination of many other related action codes involving her family and friends (see fig. 1.2). Similarly, a musical often has so many interrelated action codes that the eventual success or failure of the film's musical show may also determine the fate of the show's financial backers, the reactions of the other entertainers to the main couple's budding romance, and the many parallel character relations that have been adding variety to the story as it unfolded. The musical formula and its inscribed resolution are outlined most clearly by Rick Altman who writes that the musical's typical romantic conclusion depends on the harmony of a couple previously at odds, which simultaneously merges their once opposed value systems.[22]

The perception, isolation, and comprehension of these major story action codes depends to varying degrees upon the viewer's attention and ability. Later in this chapter we will further define the spectator, but for the moment we may posit a viewer who reaches cardinal story points, thinks back to pertinent moments within this film or similar films, and

Fig. 1.2. *All That Heaven Allows.* Cary remains
with Ron

hypothesizes about the immediate or ultimate result. In fact, Gerald
Prince also cites the spectators' active process of working toward a text's
ending, as they weigh possible results of current scenes: "Reading a
narrative is waiting for the end and the quality of that waiting is the
quality of the narrative."[23] The more quickly one can guess the outcome
of various events and of the film as a whole, the less dynamic will be the
spectator's expectation. Bordwell describes this hypothesis-making process as a narrowing of options: "We are prepared to slot actions into a
narrow 'outcome' format."[24]

A story, therefore, is comprehended as a series of interrelated
functions, indices, informants, and characters, each of which has a
varying effect on the resolution of individual scenes and on the eventual
ending. In *Band Wagon* (Minnelli, 1953), Tony Hunter and Gabrielle
Girard learn in Central Park that they can in fact dance together, which
cues the spectator to expect eventually both a successful show and a
romantic union as well. In *Casablanca* (Curtiz, 1942), the spectator
witnesses a series of events revealing that Rick can and will "stick his
neck out" for others in spite of his repeated claims. For instance, once

he helps a beautiful Bulgarian refugee find money for a visa to Lisbon, it is more likely that he will help Ilsa Lund, the woman of his dreams, leave Casablanca with her husband too. In this way, stories are made of small events, many of which may at first seem inconsequential, yet that ultimately influence major story events. Hitchcock films, for example, are often filled with objects such as cigarette lighters, eyeglasses, or attaché cases; these objects would be simple informants in some films, but here they become significant clues for the story's end result.

While every object in a film is theoretically within the realm of "story elements," not all of these elements aid in the completion of the major story actions. The resolution of a film's story requires that the driving action codes (defeating the bandits, finding a job, getting married) be completed. Thus, at the end of *Shane* (Stevens, 1953), the gunfighter has defeated the evil hired guns, won the respect of the farmers, but refused to break up Marian and Joe Starrett's marriage. By his "losing" the woman, the potential romance code is ended, simultaneously reinforcing a network of other generic and ideological conventions. As Virginia Wright Wexman writes, the sanctity of the farm / home is often privileged by classical Westerns over sexual unions that do not involve land and ownership.[25]

Yet not every story resolves its major hermeneutic codes. Italian neorealism is often praised for telling more loosely organized and less directed stories, so that characters do not always achieve what they set out to accomplish: Will Francesco ever return to Marcello in *Open City* (Rossellini, 1945)? Will Ricci of *The Bicycle Thief* (De Sica, 1949) ever obtain another bicycle? How will the family survive? A film's tale may also become so splintered that it is unclear what would be required to "complete" the story. If a film follows a group of characters, or several ill-defined ones, as in Rossellini's *Paisan* (1946), it becomes a collection of individual, variously resolved scenes rather than a resolved central story; general themes may unite and organize such a film more than actions by specific characters (and here films like *RoGoPaG*, *Paris vu par* or *New York Stories*, each composed of short films, would provide more extreme examples).

Thus, by dividing a story into character, actions, and events, we begin to identify and analyze how openness on the story level operates. Not all stories will be equally resolved since the logic of cause-effect, temporal and spatial continuity, and character behavior all influence whether there are any dominant action codes and whether those codes are finally completed. The analysis of a story's resolution allows the film critic to divide films into two large categories, those with resolved stories and those that remain comparatively unresolved. Before describing these two rather rough-hewn categories, however, it is essential to outline the second component of a filmic narrative, its narrative discourse.

Narrative Discourse

The narrative discourse is the "telling" dimension of a text—the site where the narrative voice, discursive style, and point of view operate. Narrating, according to Genette, is a process whereby a story, in varying degrees, can be told "according to one point of view or another," manipulating the spectator's perspective.[26] Genette divides narrative production into tense (story time related to discourse time), aspect (the way the story is perceived by the narrative voice), and mood (the type of discursive representation used).[27] The status of the narrative voice is one of the larger concerns of the analysis of narrative discourse; this book characterizes the narrating perspective in terms of focalization, to specify cinematic applications of Genette's concepts.

Narrative discourse involves the network of narrating systems at work within a filmic text. Included among these systems will be voice-over narration, the selection and ordering of the narrated story elements (including editing patterns), musical interventions, extratextual and intertextual insertions or references, and sound to image relations. It is via discursive production that a characterized narrative voice may be constructed, for, as Mary Ann Doane writes, "The 'voice' of the narrative does not precede and determine the discourse. Rather, the concept of voice emerges from the structure and form of the discourse."[28] In some ways, therefore, narrative discourse resembles the discours defined by Barthes since it has its own "units, its own rules, its own grammar." For any convincing textual analysis, the specific narrating systems must be investigated before the text as a whole can be understood.[29]

Our goal is to explain the necessity of testing a film's story for its degree of resolution, and checking its narrative discourse for systems of closure. Closure most often involves a stylistic framing of the text and story; it may frame the text with parallel motifs, bracket the narrative by imposing similar opening and closing elements, return to the primary narrator, and attach discursive closure devices to call an end to the narration. Parallelism helps bracket the text by maintaining constancy in the relations of the textual structures to the plotting of the story. When two related stories are resolved at the same time (like the musical show's success and the offstage romantic union of its lead performers), resolution is reinforced; simultaneously, the alternation of musical and romantic sequences helps enclose the narrating structures. By alternating parallel scenes (such as a musical's contrasting of the labor and repetition involved in musical rehearsals with the more spontaneous evolution of the love story), the text directs and unifies its narration. The discursive strategy of parallelism works closely with the story progression to create a solidly homogeneous narrative.

Bracketing by means of similar opening and closing sequences or combinations of elements allows a fiction film to maintain a cyclical unity for its narrative. Using identical situations to begin and end a film can work comically or dramatically to buckle the story into a very controlled narration. Simultaneously, such bracketing proves that the narrator knew where the story was heading all along. For instance, Tavernier's *A Sunday in the Country* (1984) opens and closes with the old painter Ladmiral contemplating his surroundings and paintings and the same shot of a tree is used at the beginning and end. Similarly, in a discussion of *Winchester 73* (Mann, 1950), Bordwell points out that film's use of a repeated opening and closing shot: "The last shot, which tracks in to a close-up of the rifle, precisely echoes the first shot of the film and indicates the return to a stable narrative situation."[30] Bracketing signals closure as a manifest narrational strategy.

Images, however, are not the only significant elements of discursive bracketing. In addition to similar shots, an opening and closing sequence may contain voice-over narration and musical themes that first establish, and then conclude their particular signifying patterns. Voice-over narration will be discussed shortly when I describe how a film returns to the voice of its primary narrator. First, however, the use of musical overtures and reprises deserves brief elaboration. Music is the most overt continuity force at work in the cinema. As Bordwell writes, "In the credits sequence, the music can lay out motifs to come, even tagging them to actors' names."[31] Music, like camera movements, identical shot composition, and credits, situates the spectator within the individual film text. After developing throughout the film, music may return as a closure device to signal the end of the narrative discourse. Bracketing a film works much like placing stylistic bookends around the story; it signals both the ending and the film's programmatic form.

The return to a primary narrator is one of the less concrete yet most successful discursive strategies used to close off the discursive production process, or *écriture*. It is a slightly abstract device since the notion of a *filmic narrator* has always been one of the trickier concepts in film studies.

22

While cinema has many of its own specific narrating codes, film studies shares several basic perspectives on narration with literary critics. Genette has worked extensively on qualifying various narrating functions, and his studies have been among the most influential for film studies: "Narration, with its narrator and narratee, fictive or not, represented or not, silent or talkative, is nonetheless continually present within what is for me . . . an act of communication." Genette is not arguing that one must adopt a strict communication theory to study narrative; rather, he emphasizes that a narrator is a construct which, as he puts it, "tells me a story, invites me to listen as it is told; and this invitation—trustworthy or pressuring—constitutes an undeniable attitude of narration, and therefore, of a narrator."[32] The presence of a narrator is always perceived by the reader or spectator in degrees, as it also occupies a wide spectrum of communicativeness. Thus, the critic's job is to ask just *how* present or absent the narrator is within each unique text.

André Gaudreault follows Genette's example by arguing that the filmic narrator can never "completely make its presence invisible, efface all the traces of its activity or the marks of its enunciation."[33] The cinematic narrator, like its literary counterpart, may take on a wide variety of personalities (each "personality" of course being perceived and assigned by the reader-viewer). While many of these analyses of the narrator remain close to linguistic models, other models also allow for an ever present, unique narrator within each narrative text. By contrast, Bordwell avoids characterizing "the filmic narrator" and instead proposes a more viewer-centered narrative model: Under certain narrative circumstances, spectators are signaled to construct a narrator. "When this occurs, we must recall that this narrator is the product of specific organizational principles, historical factors, and viewers' mental sets."[34] This approach quite accurately allows the narrator to become a product of the narration itself, instead of forcing a communication model sender-narrator to be the ultimate source of every film. Nonetheless, Bordwell does allow narration to be communicative, intimate, even deceitful, all of which will allow us to claim that viewers construct narrators out of clues from the narrative discourse.

Narration and Narrative Voice

Narration need not always be reduced to any real human entity, but a narrator, a system of narrative voices, must be built into a narrative model. Narrative voice is the constructed set of narrative cues designating the active telling of the story. Narrative discourse includes the narrative situation (first person narration, narrative point of view, narrative focalization, direct address, omniscient analytical narration), as well as the production of that narrative situation. To speak of narrative voice allows us to differentiate textual narrative (intertitles, overt or self-conscious camera movement and editing) from internal character narrators. This very distinction is one that enunciation theories cannot make, since in those theories characters may be said to "enunciate" as much as the text itself. We will speak of a narrative voice here as a group of narrative techniques, such as editing principles and musical interventions, or as an inscribed narrator; these techniques may even collectively create a definite personality or presence. In this way narrative discourse is much larger than the narrator, since it orders and produces the internal narrative systems. As Edward Branigan writes, it is best to reserve the term discourse "to refer to the totality of meaning generated by a textual system, and keep narration or enunciation to refer to that subsystem which implicates a subject in an activity: telling, watching, listening."[35]

The concept of narrative proposed here allows for the more conventional conceptions of narrator offered by critics like Genette and Prince. As Prince argues, "Every narration presupposes not only (at the very least) a narrator, but also, (at least) a *narrataire*, that is to say, someone whom the narrator is addressing."[36] While the narratee does not necessarily have to feel personally addressed, the whole definition of a narrative demands a perceiver and a narrating text. According to Prince, even a text with no overt marks of address has a zero-degree narratee: "If we consider that all narration is composed from a series of signals to a narratee, we can distinguish two large categories of signals: the *zero degree*, offering no overt marks of the narratee, and *specified* narration, which may even assign a fictional personality to both narrator and viewer."[37] The former instance would involve the bulk of classical narration, while the second, "specified" narration, drawn in literature from such clear cases as *Tristram Shandy*, could apply to films like *Will Success Spoil Rock Hunter?* (Tashlin, 1957) in which the narratee is assumed to live in 1957 and regularly watch television.

One of the most helpful concepts for understanding how a film's narrative voices may be ordered is Genette's description of narrative levels, in which every narrated instance is at one level lower than its narrator.[38] In this model, *Sunset Boulevard*'s (Wilder, 1950) extradiegetic narrator, here the fictional narrator at the highest level, is the dead Joe Gillis. Gillis is extradiegetic since he narrates all the internal material (including intradiegetic narration by other characters). When a film begins and ends with an extradiegetic narrator, the narrative discourse is constructing another of its bracketing closure devices, since a return to the framing narration (so codified in noir films like *Double Indemnity* [Wilder, 1944], or *D.O.A.* [Maté, 1950]) signals an end of the narration.

The interesting aspect of narrative levels lies in what happens before and after fictional narrators, like *Double Indemnity*'s Walter Neff, and *D.O.A.*'s Frank Bigelow, tell us their stories. Genette does not allow for a textual narrative force outside of a fictional extradiegetic narrator. My model, however, which views the narrator as a collection of narrative voices and strategies, allows for another narrative level outside the fictional narrator. This larger primary narrator is not a fictional construct: thus, while Joe Gillis would be an extradiegetic-homodiegetic narrator, the primary narrator is extradiegetic-heterodiegetic.

Primary narration is the narrative voice that opens and closes the film, reaching beyond the knowledge and capabilities of homodiegetic narrators. It is this larger heterodiegetic narrator that begins and ends the film with credit sequences, selects the non-diegetic music, and does the job of narrator in films lacking a homodiegetic narrator like Joe Gillis or Frank Bigelow. According to Genette, there is always a narrator present within a narrative, so the options open to any narrative text are whether or not the narrator should be inside or outside the diegesis, and then whether it should be overt or covert.[39] In a film like *The Quiet Man* (Ford, 1952), a character, Father Lonergan, narrates some of the tale, yet an unobtrusive primary narrator begins and ends the film, outside of Lonergan's control. However, art films typically manipulate the notion of a primary narrator, beginning and ending in a more dispersed and unconventional manner which cues the viewer to question the unity and function of the whole concept of narrator. In the beginning of Godard's *Detective* (1985), for instance, the title and credits intrude into the first quarter of the film, inserting intertitles to list characters and comment upon them ("Star—Claude Brasseur"). The varying intrusion or perceptibility of a narrator depends on the film's narrative traditions and strategies.

The fact that a film is indeed constructed does demand that there be a narrator. A rock is an object found in nature, but once it is filmed in a close-up for *Weekend*, lighting, shot scale, angle, film stock, and the soundtrack re-present it (see fig. 1.3). A fiction film is not a found object and any representation allows the spectator to recreate a narrative activity or narrator to varying degrees. Narrative voices, then, are systems of narration isolated by the spectator during and after the film. As we will see, a classical film like *The Quiet Man* has a relatively codified collection of narrative voices, all of which serve the efficient narration of Sean Thornton's return to Ireland. On the other hand, Godard's *Weekend* and *Tout va bien* (1972), cue us to isolate very overt and even conflicting narrative voices at work within a single text. The degree to which the narrative strategies of these films aid or avoid discursive closure plays an instrumental role in their overall stories and especially their ends.

The primary narrator, therefore, is the controlling voice constructed by the spectator out of organizational cues from the narrative and finally brackets the text. This bracketing function operates on a large textual level, using textual and paratextual codes to address the spectator, begin the narrative, and eventually close off the narrative and the text. Thus, the dedication of *The 400 Blows* to the memory of André Bazin works along with the opening music and travelling shots to prepare the spectator for a lyrical film dealing with sentiment, memory,

Fig. 1.3. *Weekend.* A rock in the hand: *re*presented

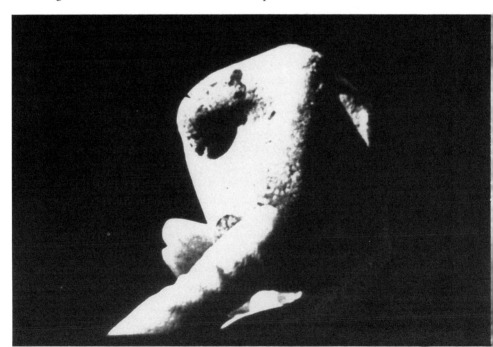

and France of the late 1950s. By contrast, the paratactic intertitles of *Weekend* that announce the "end of cinema" proceed from very different functions, yet each film employs a primary narrator at its beginning and ending. The primary narrative voice operates at the highest, most extradiegetic level of the text, and strongly influences the viewer's comprehension of the start and end, which leads us to a brief consideration of just what a viewer's task in analysis of narration might be.

The Spectator

One of the biggest challenges in the definition of a filmic viewer is the fact that several of the most prominent trends in theory are related to such dynamic fields as psychoanalysis and cognitive psychology. As a result, concrete models of spectating are partially based on systems of knowledge which are themselves in the process of constant upheaval and re-development. There are also immediate problems for film studies given that the bulk of narrative theory refers to a literary or reading audience rather than an audio-visual viewer. Literature's reader is constantly compared to film's spectator, with many critical models assuming an equivalence between the comprehension of various media. Semiotics, based on a linguistic notion of meaning production of semiotic systems, has too often collapsed the roles of reader and film spectator, partially resulting in a cyclical self-sustaining definition. Obviously, there are many similar mental processes at work within narrative comprehension no matter what the medium. However, collapsing literary and cinematic perception and understanding into a unified process known only as *reading* does a disservice to notions of semiotic specificity regarding cinematic codes and their comprehension.

The central issue in the delineation of a film spectator concerns the problem of isolating how meaning is ultimately produced in the individual. A second, related task is to hypothesize how narrative and the cinema interrelate with regard to basic thought processes. This second stage is one which should be based on some model of meaning acquisition and production. In the end, therefore, a workable model of spectating must incorporate all the mental activities, conscious and unconscious, of the typical individual subject; the model must then relate those mental processes to the cinematic apparatus in general, and eventually to specific film experience. Thus, a narrative model implies a model of human perception and thinking which is ultimately beyond the scope of the average film or literary critic. Finally, the structure sought by narrative theory is precisely the structure of human thought.

One approach to defining a workable model of spectatorship is to establish the various functions and characteristics which must be accounted for by a spectator theory. The film spectator must be able to perceive the film images and sounds, comprehend those images and sounds, and relate the events, characters, and settings to past experience within the same film or across intertextual boundaries. The most productive conception of a spectator, therefore, will be one that can account for how people process the cinematic elements into an understanding of a story, and then also account for how the viewer relates cinematic techniques to meaning.

Todorov has isolated four stages of narrative comprehension, adapted from Bakhtin's writings, that act as a helpful beginning for our discussion of what a narrative theory must consider in its definition of an audience. The first step to comprehension is the psycho-physiological perception of the material sign (a word, color, sound, or spatial form). The second stage is the spectator's "recognition" of the sign as either known or unknown. This second part results in "reiterable signification" of the specific sign. Third, there is "the comprehension of its signification within the given context." The fourth stage is an active dialogical comprehension: "The moment of evaluation with the comprehension and the degree of its depth and universality."[40] These operations must be accounted for in relation to cinematically specific terms and codes.

Todorov and Bakhtin's theorization of perception and comprehension actually lead toward a constructivist theory of viewing wherein perceiving and thinking are goal-oriented processes. One of the leading contemporary theorists of perception and meaning is David Bordwell who writes that the viewer makes sense of a film by asking mental questions: "Through criteria of verisimilitude (is x plausible?), of generic appropriateness (is x characteristic of this sort of film?) and of compositional unity (does x advance the story?)."[41] This schema of viewing closely resembles many models since the semiotic reader is also conceived as testing textual progress by asking questions, be they hermeneutic, referential, symbolic, or extratextual.

The spectator must, therefore, be theorized as perceiving images and sounds which can then be related to each other and to other textual experiences. The spectator requires both perceptual skills and interpretational strategies, both of which depend upon memory and hypothesis-making. In this way, the reading activities, including perception, sign identification, hypothesis-making, and filling in narrative gaps in order to guess what comes next, all become crucial for any study of how spectators interpret a film's ending. The ultimate hypothesis anticipates the ending.

Thus, the spectator reads, views, and interprets, since spectating implies a semiotic, rather than narrowly linguistic, activity. We can gain quite productively from Francesco Casetti's definition of a spectator who decodes, interprets, and constructs the narrative:

> By connecting sparse cues in order to build up a character or place; by providing a framework in which the data are given their full value (e.g. suggestiveness of genre labels); by scanning visual patterns within the frame to grasp the essential and discard the unimportant; by filling the gaps in the narrative to restore the completeness of the story (frequently, the unseen is essential in explaining what seems manifest). The viewer lives in the film. . . . The spectator *commits* him/herself to viewing.[42]

This spectator is not a simple, ideologically determined viewer, but one who is conscious of his or her role in determining meaning both within and outside of the textual codes.

For this study, the most important aspect of the spectator is how s/he works toward the film's ending, and how that ending satisfies the viewing process. The degree of resolution of the story and closure of the narrative discourse both depend upon the viewer's interpretations of the end. Smith summarizes the reader's activity as helping to determine the degree and appropriateness of the text's conclusion; therefore the completeness of a text depends on the viewer's acceptance and perception of that completeness: "Our sense of completeness of form depends upon the class of forms with which we identify it."[43] When Shane rides off into the distance, the story is in some ways left unresolved, yet this ending is a very typical generic closure device. Judged against a musical like *Band Wagon*, *Shane* has a certain degree of irresolution ("Where is he going now?"); when that same ending is set beside the end of *My Darling Clementine* (Ford 1946), it appears perfectly closed and even clichéd (see figs. 1.4 and 1.5).

The spectating process itself, built on the forward progression of hypothesis-making, memory, and intertextual comparisons, resembles the semiotic model of both syntagmatic and paradigmatic ordering. Horst Ruthrof characterizes literary cognition by the "forward reading direction's" relation to the text's depth.[44] The reader's progression through the text ultimately leads to a narrower "horizon of expecta-

Fig. 1.4. *Band Wagon*. Gabrielle Girard and the company thank Tony Hunter

Fig. 1.5. *My Darling Clementine*. Wyatt Earp says good-bye to Clementine

tions," according to Ruthrof. "It is during our reading that this set is then transformed into a cumulative list of aspects which, by the end of our first reading, make up our understanding of the work."[45] This process depends as much on what *has* happened as what *will* happen in the narrative. Thus the spectator must proceed both by expectation and retrospection in the viewing of any film text.

Retrospection has been outlined by both Barbara Herrnstein Smith and Shlomith Rimmon-Kenan in their accounts of how reading proceeds and eventually even rethinks its own process. Smith, working from shorter poetic texts, sees "retrospective patterning" as a component of textual endings: "Connections and similarities are illuminated, and the reader perceives that seemingly gratuitous or random events, details and juxtapositions have been selected in accord with certain principles."[46] The end allows for, or even demands, the viewer's reconsideration of prior motifs or events. Mystery and detective films often include some revelation that previously held hypotheses were incomplete or incorrect. For example, *Brazil*'s (Gilliam, 1985) surprise ending reveals that the happy ending we had thought to be "real" was (probably) a subjective fantasy. It is important to realize, however, that retrospection is a constant activity and does not surface only at the close of a narrative.

Thus, film viewing is a double process involving expectation and retrospection, and is determined by textual cues as well as the particular background required of the spectator by the individual film. The end becomes a dynamic location for meaning acquisition and the testing of spectating assumptions. Kermode refers to an acceleration of viewer choices as the text progresses, until "the final end begins to exert a gravitational pull."[47] One of the initial reasons for this study of closure in the cinema was an interest in how diverse narrative traditions manipulate the degree of this expectation of a certain ending. The more classical genre films constantly reaffirm viewer expectations, even if they play at threatening the eventual likelihood of the typical ending; many other less formulaic films, however, really do overturn our expectations and even baffle us.

The spectator in this study will be important in that each of my four categories of endings uses different strategies of storytelling, and thus each requires different spectating functions. While the classical film's spectator is just as "active" as the other films' spectators, s/he will be expected to make different sorts of assumptions and follow different kinds of textual codes—some quite linear, others quite circuitous. It is

31

worth reiterating, therefore, that the viewer is the ultimate force in determining the processes of narration at work in films.

While openings are very richly privileged moments in a film's address to the spectator, the ending is the final product of all the narrative's labors—the end is privileged both during and after the viewing as a source of validation of the reading process. The spectator is prepared for a certain degree of resolution and closure and given to expect a possible termination point. When that point is reached, it may have to be retroactively justified by the spectator (particularly in the case of "surprise" endings, such as *The Lady Vanishes* [Hitchcock, 1938], or *The Crying Game* [Jordon, 1992]); the viewer is then forced to rethink earlier scenes. Whereas a film's first shots are scanned for clues about what major action codes will be opening, the last shots are read for their anchoring proof and condensed summary of all the codes that were set in motion within the text as a whole. The ending stands as the final address to the spectator, the place where the story may be resolved and where the narrative discourse may close. All of these elements are subject to the perception and interpretation of the spectator, for, as Armine Kotin Mortimer writes, "Readers cannot possess a story's meaning until they know the end."[48]

The Categories

This detour through the theorization of endings and their functions for the narrative and spectator alike helps set the stage for the study that follows. Rather than organize my claims around catalogues of various sorts of endings, I offer a rigorous format that allows us to understand better the very operation of filmic narration and the relation of how stories and narration proceed and finally conclude. The novelty of my analyses lies precisely in the efficient grid of four large narrational options for all fictional films. If we can accept that some films will have stories that are more resolved than others (*The Quiet Man* vs. *The Bicycle Thief* for instance) and that some discursive strategies provide more closure than others (*The Quiet Man* vs. Alain Robbe-Grillet's *L'Immor-telle*, 1963), then we can logically and productively posit four possible categories of narrative film endings: First, in the classical *Closed Text* film, story is resolved and discourse is closed; Second, in the *Open Story* film, the story is left unresolved but the narrative discourse is closed; Third, in the *Open Discourse* film, the story is resolved but the narrative discourse avoids strict closure of its strategies; Fourth, the *Open Text* leaves both narrative levels open. The latter three categories thereby challenge classical notions of resolution, completeness, or even unity in ever more dramatic and radical ways. The options can also be represented as a grid:

	Closed Narrative Discourse	Open Narrative Discourse
Resolved Story	1) Closed Text	3) Open Discourse
Unresolved Story	2) Open Story	4) Open Text

All texts do end in a material way: the last shot may be superimposed with a "the end" title, the lights come up in the theater, and we leave our seats. But the degree of closure and resolution at the end of a Robbe-Grillet or Godard film is much lower than at the end of a generic romantic comedy or even a neorealist tale. This book's overall purpose is to shift attention away from only considering plot lines and ambiguity when we discuss how films end, to paying closer attention to the relations between narration and story for how both dimensions of a filmic text cue, or as Bordwell would say, "train" the spectator to play the game according to its specific ground rules. These four categories are outlined and proposed here to lend the film critic tools for evaluating and detailing the interwoven processes of narration and viewing, and beginning and ending that make narratives, as Metz's opening quote points out, unlike the real world which, one hopes, does not finally end.

THE CLOSED TEXT FILM

Because spectators see the same scenarios in so many films,
they have become good scenarists and can always foretell
what's coming and how it's going to end.
—François Truffaut[1]

The Closed Text film has the most secure ending of the four groups and
satisfies conventional demands for unity and resolution. Closed Text
films are historically dominant because their narrative modes derive
from classical traditions; they have also proven commercially successful.
Literary figures from Walter Benjamin and Jean-Paul Sartre to Hayden
White and Peter Brooks have argued that solid closure in conventional
narratives and histories satisfies individual and social desire for moral
authority, a purposeful interpretation of life, and genuine stability, all
of which stand in sharp contrast to the chance and alterity in the world
around us. Elizabeth MacArthur echoes such arguments when she
writes that closure represents "an attempt to preserve the moral and
social order which would be threatened by endlessly erring narratives."[2]
It is no wonder that the commercial classical Hollywood cinema, whose
"happy endings" become an overly codified norm, should adhere to
conventional closure so wholeheartedly.

Closed Text films boost their degree of completeness by having
each level of textual production (story and narrative discourse) reinforce what the other level is doing. An archetypal ending of a Hollywood Western, for instance, may include a swelling reprise of the
film's theme music, which is accompanied by a crane shot rising up to

isolate the lone gunfighter riding off into the sunset. While this sort of ending has become a comical cliché, open to parody in films like *Blazing Saddles* (Brooks, 1974), it clearly exhibits the interlacing of the story's resolution (the cowboy having accomplished his mission can now move on to another place and challenge) with discursive closure devices (the camerawork isolates the retreating rider, a musical reprise swells, and there is a slow fade to black) (see fig 1.5 of *My Darling Clementine*). A Closed Text need not be so predictably generic however. The story and discourse in *Citizen Kane* (Welles, 1941) also provide interdependent resolution and closure. The narrative logic is that story resolution is completed and reinforced by discursive devices that signal the film's end and produce a stable product, the Closed Text film. According to Armine Kotin Mortimer, "The concept of narrative closure generally depends on a feeling of satisfaction that the story's elements ended at their necessary spot, problems posed are resolved . . . in sum, what was opened is now closed."[3] Thus, the textually inscribed desires for story, form, and social order are perfectly satisfied within Closed Text films.

This chapter examines the degree to which classical films can be said to have "predetermined" endings or at least termination points. Peter Brooks argues that the conventional novel is organized as "a chain of moments driven by desire to the quiescence and coherent significance of closure." He adds that as we proceed through a narrative we assume and even depend upon the notion that what remains to be seen will provide further significance to the provisional meanings of what we have *already* seen.[4] Similarly, many film critics underline the unity of the classical cinema, claiming that an ending is already clearly contained in the film's beginning. To a certain extent, of course, this may be true, but we need to look more closely before deciding whether the classical text is so repetitious that its opening can be said to reveal its ending. We must also consider what such predictability would do to and for spectatorship and narrative form.

Because the narrative cinema grew out of turn-of-the-century theatrical and literary traditions, films accepted or acquired many of their long established aesthetic constraints. As Marc Vernet notes, the cinema had to prove it was as worthy as "the noble arts." For example, while even the earliest programs by Georges Méliès were already stories, they still did not possess the developed, complex forms of a play or novel.[5] As we discuss the Closed Text, therefore, we must examine the influence other narrative media and their norms hold on the cinema, beginning with a brief analysis of the central role characters play in the text's overall logic and structure.

Character action has traditionally motivated and organized plot. As Ann Jefferson explains, "In the European novel of the nineteenth century the *telos* of fiction was largely provided by character, which took precedence over plot as the basis of artistic coherence."[6] Kristin Thompson has thoroughly argued that the cinema gained its models for characterization from vaudeville, drama, the short story, and the novel as film learned to balance narrative unity, character action and psychological delineation.[7] Thus, saying that classical films are built around character progression risks appearing too obvious to mention. Yet, as we define the Closed Text, we may productively connect the motivating role of character with Seymour Chatman's observation that traditional plots are constructed around active instances of problem solving.[8]

The most efficient portrayal of character and plot development leads into a chain of character actions; the classical film thus becomes an ongoing series of segment-to-segment movements until the final conclusive segment is revealed. One critic who has succinctly linked character to plot advancement is David Bordwell: "Once defined as an individual through traits and motifs, the character assumes a causal role because of his or her desires . . . The hero desires something new . . . or the hero seeks to restore an original state."[9] The link between character goals and story structure thereby produces what Thierry Kuntzel calls "the classic sequence," which "presents itself as a narratively and formally autonomous, detachable and self-sufficient segment. *At the same time*, it is a link in a chain: the action which . . . ends from the point of view of the sequence, opens a new action, from the point of view of the entire narrative."[10] The goal-oriented classical character's progress, proceeding as a series of successes or delays, unifies the classical narrative's time, space, and plot while eventually providing one or more termination points.

The Closed Text story also owes much of its unity to intertwined plot lines and rhyming structures. Typically, a narrative structure sets up a series of cardinal story functions, and then keeps all the plot lines parallel or interrelated. In this way, the narrative supports its own story logic so that Tony Hunter's Broadway show in *Band Wagon* is a great success (rewarding his artistic intuition) so he then wins his dancing partner, Gabrielle Girard, away from her much younger dance teacher. Similarly, Shane's skill in overcoming the hired guns is paralleled by his stimulation of wife/mother Marian Starrett's desire. Thus, here too, there is a double resolution inscribed right from the start: First, *Shane*'s segments routinely open (Shane shows young Joey how to shoot) and conclude (Joe Starrett scolds Shane and Marian becomes more troubled by Shane's presence) as the film progresses. Second, the completion of these mini-story sequences joins the parallel plot lines (the need to fight to protect land and family, and Shane's growing influence over Joey and Marian) which are in turn working toward *their* own endings. Finally, Shane proves himself superior to Joe Starrett and the hired gun Wilson in strength, but he squelches Joey and Marian's desire by leaving the Starrett family intact. In both films a controlling rhyme structure heads ineluctably toward a very complete and unified resolution, although only the conclusion to *Band Wagon* happily "creates the couple" to use Virginia Wright Wexman's term (see fig. 1.4). *Shane*, by contrast, reinforces generic norms in an unusual way by attaching *two* conventional termination points at once: *Shane* guarantees a future complete with land and his family for the hard-working Joe Starrett, while Shane rides off into the sunset, reinforcing his own eternal, masculine isolation.[11] Both films also remain true to generic form; the musical-comedy protagonist by definition must win, and the westerner must settle down, die, or move on.[12]

The emphasis on character action and carefully limited time and space allows the classical cinema, like the realistic novel, to embed itself within a codified diegesis that lends a sort of self-induced and plausible predestination to its actions and events. The resulting plausibility, as defined by Christian Metz, functions textually but also culturally and intertextually because outside influences determine what is logical or plausible for the specific era, genre, or text: "Thus, from its inception, the Plausible is a reduction of real possibles, it is an *arbitrary* and *cultural* restriction of real possibles; it is, in fact, censorship."[13] As Mary Ann Doane argues, the result of this plausible containment, its resulting unity is that classical narratives enclose and thus sustain their own represented worlds.[14] Generic conventions only serve to limit possible conclusions; as Thomas Schatz points out, generic resolution arrives "in a fashion which eliminates the physical and/or ideological threat and thereby clebrates the (temporarily) well-ordered community."[15]

While the Closed Text's story struggles to limit and direct itself toward the eventual resolution of its structuring plot lines, its narrative discourse labors to relate that story via devices that will conclude the film definitively when the story is completed. One such closure device is the presence of a large framing structure that allows the end to mirror or respond to the film's beginning in a sort of bookend construction. Minnelli's *Gigi* (1958) is a clear example of a film that uses similar opening and closing scenes to bracket the text's narration. Moreover, Bellour uses *Gigi*'s structure as representative of the way a classical text controls itself via repetition and rhyming. In *Gigi*, the narrative discourse is closed by the return of Honoré (Maurice Chevalier) to the same location in the Bois de Boulogne where the film began. This time a young couple appears and, as Bellour notes, it is the solution of the narrative's enigma: Gigi is now accompanied by her husband Gaston.[16] Gigi's progression from the schoolgirl of the opening scene, to the wife of the epilogue, combines with the repetition of setting and situation to supply archetypal examples of the couple's creation in the story and unified closure of the discourse.

In addition to this bracketing, *Gigi* also employs a single dominant voice narrating the story. In *Gigi*, the intradiegetic narrator, Honoré, addresses the spectator directly at the beginning and end, giving a concrete source for the tale. When Honoré concludes the film with his philosophical insights and a final rendition of "Thank Heaven for Little Girls," he accomplishes what every Closed Text attempts: he wraps up the film's narrative strategies, putting an end to its discursive production. Once he stops singing and the non-diegetic music continues, the narrative control returns to the unseen primary narrator's control.

Similarly, Spike Lee's *Do the Right Thing* (1989) employs a mirroring structure to rhyme the opening and closing sections while reinforcing character developments. At the beginning Mookie counts his money, wakes up his sister, and goes to Sal's to work and ask for an advance on his salary. At the end, Mookie wakes up with his girlfriend Tina, then he heads down to Sal's burned out store to ask for and receive his pay. Other narrative repetitions, such as the radio DJ and references to the weather, bracket the rhyming structure as well, however, the film's larger thematic, rhetorical function—to point to the very real challenges remaining in both the diegetic and referential worlds—remains unresolved. Wexman privileges such ideological issues over story and discourse and finds a lively tension results: "That the film's final scene of reconciliation takes place between Mookie and Sal rather than Mookie and Tina points to its concern with the economic base on which social mores such as romantic love are based. . . . The result of the exchange between Sal and Mookie is ambiguous . . . and thus it does not provide a classical sense of closure."[17] Wexman's point is that the film opens up larger questions in a Brechtian manner. However the fact that a text may impose story resolution and closure while its narration cues us to notice larger ideological questions that have been overtly or covertly left for further debate and consideration hardly violates classical norms. Spike Lee's films, especially *Do the Right Thing* and *Jungle Fever* (1991), challenge the audience to confront larger extratextual issues that the films touch upon but fail to "settle."

There are other strategies for bracketing a text and returning to a stable, dominant primary narrator. One option involves beginning the story in the present, then offering the body of the story as one or more flashbacks, and finally returning to the present time period at the film's close. This pattern is illustrated by *Le Jour se lève* (Carné, 1939) which begins with François (Jean Gabin), shooting Valentin (Jules Berry), and then tells the story as three flashbacks, leading up to the opening scene, and eventually concluding with François's suicide (see fig. 2.1). As Maureen Turim writes, "The structure of Carné's film reverses cause and effect order, giving us the effect, murder, first, and the cause, an overwhelming psychic tension, following that." In the end, the double temporal structure lends an "increasingly pessimistic progression of events within the 'causal' segments."[18] This plot reversal, so popular among films noir such as *The Killers* (Siodmak, 1946) and *Out of the Past* (Tourneur, 1947), guarantees the story's resolution from the start, while the return to a previously established time and place reinstates the opening discursive positions and privileges a classical hierarchy of narrative voices.

The labor of the classical film to create this unified termination effect has come under study for both its ideological and narrative effects. According to Steve Neale, for instance, the absence of other challenging levels of narrative discourse in a text prevents the narrative from acknowledging the subjectivity of this film's dominant and final "truth."[19] Similarly, Martin Sutton observes that musical comedies generally end in marriage, yet "the word 'marriage' will have to be taken in a wider sense to include the 'wedding' of culturally accepted oppositions."[20] The happy ending is especially subject to these analyses since, as Jacques Aumont writes, "The *happy ending* is a micro-structure of the narrative, and as such, hypercodified—but it is *also* the necessary form for an ideology of reconciliation."[21]

Within the classical film, this successful team work between story and narration is not only a sign of efficiency, but proof of proficiency as well. Therefore, this chapter investigates how a Closed Text film produces such a logical, directed, and efficient conclusion to its narrative production. John Ford's *The Quiet Man* (1952) is our representative Closed Text film. There are several reasons behind the selection of this Ford film: First, while *The Quiet Man* does stand as a strong example of classical Hollywood production, it does not belong to a narrow film genre. My selection of this romance rather than a Western, musical, or film noir, sidesteps the risk of being limited to the conventions of a particular genre. Second, while *The Quiet Man* is the work of Ford, a recognized "auteur," this film has not been studied as often as many other Ford classics. Third, *The Quiet Man* employs a voice-over narration that allows us to test more fully the notions of primary and secondary narration as part of the text's discursive strategies.

Story Resolution in *The Quiet Man*

The Quiet Man serves as an excellent example of Closed Text since the film's story and structure make the production of a very secure ending playfully obvious. This film makes manifest what all Closed Texts attempt—it completes all the major story events and actions, while simultaneously building a discursive structure to conclude the film with an epilogue as closure device. Thus, while not all Closed Texts are as blatantly self-conscious in their endings, all Closed Texts will, in one way or another, have endings that accomplish the same functions. Their resolution, coupled with secure closure, returns the viewer to a pleasurable spectating position.

In the analysis of *The Quiet Man*, I refer to a shot-by-shot breakdown (Appendix A) that divides the film into thirty-one sequences. While that segmentation provides a very detailed plot summary, we may here simply condense the story as follows: Sean Thornton, an ex-boxer from America, returns to the Irish village Innisfree where he was born (see fig. 2.2). He buys his old home from the Widow Tillane, thereby angering neighbor Will Danaher who not only wants to buy the same property, but would use it to link his land with that of the Widow, whom he secretly desires. Will is further angered that his sister Mary Kate and Sean begin courting and finally marry, and Will refuses to give her the dowry he promised. To get the money and earn Mary Kate's respect, Sean must publicly humiliate Will and shame Mary Kate by returning her (see fig. 2.3). Will gives them the money, which Mary Kate and Sean then burn, which leads to a fistfight between the men (see fig. 2.4). Sean has learned that in Ireland a man sometimes must fight to earn the respect of those around him; his "homeric" fistfight with Will is even encouraged and cheered by Will's priest Father Lonergan and Sean's Pastor Playfair.

41

Fig. 2.1. *Le Jour se lève*. François turns the gun
on himself

Fig. 2.2. *The Quiet Man*. Sean arrives and asks how
to get to Innisfree

Fig. 2.3. Sean returns Mary Kate to Will Danaher

Fig. 2.4. Sean and Mary Kate burn the dowry money

Once Sean clobbers Will he wins Mary Kate's true affection and devotion and is finally welcomed into Innisfree by everyone; the whole village can finally "breathe easier" as Father Lonergan says. Moreover, a bandaged Will finally shares Michaleen Og Flynn's courting cart with the Widow Tillane, guaranteeing a second marriage.

In order to illustrate how efficient the film's storytelling is, my analysis begins with segment 30, in which Will Danaher and Sean Thornton return, drunk and tired, to the waiting Mary Kate Danaher. After the Reverend and Mrs. Playfair settle their accounts over the betting on Will and Sean's fight, there is a dissolve into segment 30, shot 742. This segment begins with a long shot of Will and Sean, arm in arm, stumbling home and singing the recurring "The Wild Colonial Boy" (see fig. 2.5). The camera follow-pans left to show that they are approaching Sean's cottage, White O'Morn. In this single shot are condensed the resolutions of many of the film's actions and character developments: While the spectator has already seen the outcome of the fight (Sean knocked Will through Cohan's Bar door), the real payoff is still to come: Sean and Will become friends and acknowledge each other as worthy brothers-in-law, and Mary Kate, instead of dining with Sean, acts like a proud mother and then dutiful maid, and serves the two men their dinners (see fig. 2.6).

If *The Quiet Man*'s central hermeneutic simply involved Sean's need to gain of his bride's fortune and respect, however, the film could have ended in segment 17 when Sean and Mary Kate throw Will's dowry money into the fire and walk off arm in arm. Instead, the creation of Sean and Mary Kate as a happy couple is not resolved until Sean and *Will* are arm in arm, signifying that Sean has now won the respect of everyone in Innisfree by proving himself rightfully part of the Danaher clan. Thus, Sean's real victory does not occur until he has defeated Will, "the best man in Innisfree." In addition, the fight proves that Sean has overcome his traumatic fear of fighting brought on by killing his last opponent (see fig. 2.7). Thus Sean's return to Ireland has been a *cure* forcing him to recover from having killed a man in the ring as a prize fighter. Sean learns that Ireland expects fights too, but here they are fought for very different reasons and rewards; instead of money, fighting in Ireland earns him a wife, land, and community, and provides what Wexman labels male "dynastic nostalgia," commonly found in Westerns, where a happy end for the man means family and land.[22]

Will Danaher is Sean's only real obstacle throughout the film, delaying and complicating Sean's pursuit of Mary Kate, White O'Morn,

Fig. 2.5. Sean and Will cross the brook after the fight

Fig. 2.6. Mary Kate sees the men approaching

Fig. 2.7. Sean in the boxing ring

Fig. 2.8. Train people ponder Sean's arrival

Fig. 2.9. Sean explains to Michaleen why he
returned

Fig. 2.10. Father Lonergan forces Sean and Will to
shake hands

and an idyllic happy life in Innisfree. Sean's physical and personal victory over Will removes the last roadblock to two major hermeneutic codes in the story: First, Sean came to Innisfree to forget his tragic past by regaining the innocence of his homeland, which he does by winning the friendship of all those living in Innisfree. Second, however, he came to recreate his family, but could only obtain his wife, Mary Kate Dana-her, by winning her brother's respect and friendship. The film's herme-neutic codes elucidate the efficient opening of this Closed Text film. In *The Quiet Man*'s second segment there is a line of people at the train station (including an often present, but never identified "motherly" woman) watching Sean drive off with Michaleen Og Flynn, while one man asks aloud for all of us, "I wonder now, why a man would go to Innisfree?" (The question of course contains its own answer since to be in In-is-free is to be free) (see fig. 2.8). The question is restated in the very next sequence as Michaleen asks why a Yankee from Pittsburgh would want to buy that "wee humble cottage," and Sean finally answers what we already suspect from his dead mother's subjective voice-over: "Because I'm Sean Thornton and I was born in that little place over there. I've come home and home I'm going to stay" (see fig. 2.9).

The spectator's questions, like those posed by the characters are thus provisionally answered, yet owning the cottage will be accom-plished by scene 6, so this chain of events involving returning home must entail more than buying back family land. Ownership of the land, just like marriage to Mary Kate, will not adequately resolve the story. Instead, total assimilation into the local society and culture (by the accompanying repression and rejection of his American past) are Sean Thornton's real goals. Will Danaher, established throughout as the obstacle to Sean's assimilation, works as a cluster of problems. First, Will is the competition for White o'Morn, but he is easily outbid by Sean. Second, when Will is in Cohan's Bar he tells Sean to stay away from Mary Kate, then wants to fight Sean, but instead is forced by Father Lonergan to shake hands (see fig. 2.10). This hand-shaking match foreshadows Sean's ability to stand up to Will physically, as they each appear impressed by the other's strength.

This scene at Cohan's Bar shows the repetition so common to classic texts, since it acts as a key nodal instance condensing actions that will reverberate and be worked out through the text as a whole: The Church (Law and Father) aids Sean; the village patriarch, an old man with a white beard who knew Sean's grandfather, welcomes Sean just as all the townspeople now will; Cohan's Bar will be the place of several skirmishes in the future between Will and Sean; and of course, it is the setting for the final punch of the fight. The music of this sequence, "The Wild Colonial Boy," identifies Sean with the song's protagonist, Jack Duggan, and since this song frames the handshake and is sung by the other men, it eventually returns to be sung by Will and Sean, sealing their relationship after the fight. One additional element of this scene is that it ends without the two opponents really settling anything; hence it prepares us for a series of conflicts between the men, while paving the way for Sean's need to fight for Mary Kate a second time to resolve all conflicts. This scene simultaneously challenges Sean to come to terms with the conflict between his own desire never to fight again, and the social custom demanding a brawl. Thus, this scene fits Kuntzel's model of closing off a smaller action, while opening the door for a future, concluding event.

As protagonist, Sean is closely tied into all the characters' goals, but his own goals organize and motivate most of the story events. Sean wants to regain his family's position and acquire the peace he expects from this place his mother called heaven on earth. In order to be accepted he needs a home, a wife, and a role other than "foreigner" in that society. He can only be happy when assimilated, and that status is eventually underlined and repeated in the final two sequences of the film. Another plot motif, referred to by shot 742, is the crossing of the Kabrook. This stream was where Sean first recognized his home, when he stopped on the bridge with Michaleen and heard his dead mother's voice describe what he, and the spectator, were seeing. Later the stream served as a colorful setting for the lonely and angry Sean to ride his horse through, then for Mary Kate to run through when she courts Sean. Eventually the brook is the spot where the fishing Father Lonergan scolds Mary Kate, telling her that in Ireland a husband sleeps in a bed and not in a bag. By the time that Will and Sean stumble through the water as friends, the shot condenses, refers to, and completes all of these earlier functions.

In the second shot of sequence 30, Mary Kate can be seen looking out of the door (see fig. 2.6). But this shot does not fit the story resolution so much as it serves the narrative discourse's closure. We will return to this scene shortly to prove that Mary Kate's perception and attention, localized in her intense, obsessive looks toward Sean, are an ordering force with specific figurative functions in the film. Here the shot relays both the story information of Mary Kate's pleasure in seeing both men returning home as friends, but also her sudden shock as she turns inside to the hearth in order to change character roles, switching from the wild, young fiancée/sister to a loving wife/mother.

The third shot of sequence 30 continues to anchor the motifs, actions, and events whose significance has accumulated throughout the text. In this shot, Mary Kate looks off left out of the cottage door, smiling in pleasant amazement until she realizes she must feed Will; she then quickly sets another chair at the table as they arrive. This camera position, in medium shot, is familiar by now, showing the outside door at frame left, the bedroom door in the background, and the fireplace at the right. This framing recalls the earlier uses of the same camera position which revealed the progress of Sean and Mary Kate's sexual relations. The first time we were inside the cottage, with Mary Kate secretly sweeping out the house, this framing was used for their first, wind-blown embrace. The next time is in sequence 18, when Sean kicks in the bedroom door and throws her on the bed, followed by the morning when Mary Kate looks outside to see her furniture arriving, but then begs Sean to hide his sleeping bag. Later, from this window/door, Mary Kate will see the new horse and buggy Sean has bought her, signifying a new level of Sean's devotion and patience.

While the window is actively significant in this shot, the fireplace is also a dynamic story element. The night after Sean and Mary Kate have spoken with Father Lonergan and Rev. Playfair, they sit together in front of the fire, and it is finally used for romance instead of cooking (see fig. 2.11). But in the morning (segment 26), Sean has to look out the door to learn from Michaleen that Mary Kate has left for Dublin in shame (see fig. 2.12). The return to this framing of Mary Kate in sequence 30, resolves the marriage—Sean brings Will home, proving it really is a home now, and Mary Kate plays the role of wife, sister, and servant while Sean flings his cap in the open bedroom door showing that he is now in control of every room in his house. This shot helps resolve the story chain of Sean and Mary Kate's marriage, but it also serves as a discursive marker or closure device due to its repetition. The film could possibly end on this shot of the two men sitting down to a dinner served by the now legitimate wife. However, too many other story events have been left open and we still expect stronger closure, in the person of Father Lonergan's framing voice-over, to conclude the film.

Predictably, the next and final scene, 31, ties together all the important character events which have not yet been settled. In this last sequence, Rev. Playfair is cheered by the village's entire population, thus ensuring his job there. Will and the Widow Sarah Tillane are then

Fig. 2.11. Sean and Mary Kate by the fireplace

Fig. 2.12. Morning: Michaleen tells Sean that Mary
Kate has left him

shown to be engaged, as they are driven down the same bridge by Michaleen Flynn. If the union of the couple is a common termination point in the classical Hollywood cinema, however, one may ask why *The Quiet Man* joins together the elements of the controlling hermeneutic (Sean's winning of Mary Kate and the town's respect) *before* all the minor action codes (Rev. Playfair's future and the Widow Tillane's engagement to Will). The answer is in the nature of the story: the engagement of Will and Widow Tillane, and even the happiness of Rev. Playfair, depend on the larger good fortune of Sean and Mary Kate.

Sean and Will's fight across the countryside breaks down barriers that have been constructed throughout the film, including the blockage of Will and the Widow's mutual attraction and the religious conflicts. While Father Lonergan displaced an earlier fight between Will and Sean in the Cohan Bar, rerouting it into a handshake, the eventual fight reveals that both Rev. Playfair and Father Lonergan see the battle as healthy and necessary, since Playfair bets on Sean, and Lonergan feigns to be boxing himself. In its truly efficient storytelling, *The Quiet Man* sets up two religious figures and shows each of them to be interested in boxing, thus they condone and even encourage Sean's fight as a necessary cultural rite. Furthermore, Rev. Playfair knows it is necessary for Sean to fight once again to overcome the trauma of having killed a man in the ring; he makes sure Sean learns that he can now fight out of duty and even respect without feeling the impulse to kill. Only after the apocalyptic fight can Mrs. Tillane marry Will. Similarly, it is only after Mary Kate's family is reestablished and happy that she and Sean are truly married. Sean's disruption of Innisfree must be shown to be beneficial to everyone in the long run for a secure happy story ending. The linking of Sean and Mary Kate's happiness to that of Will and Tillane, allows the story to create two happy couples where before there were none.

The final sequence rewards these secondary characters, resolves all the interdependent storylines, and adds the generic comical resolution of a community in celebration. All the characters from the film, including the motherly woman of the opening shot, the Castletown train people, and the IRA members, are gathered together in one last mythical social ritual; they salute Rev. Playfair, observe the courting of Will and Widow Tillane, and hail the reunion of Sean and Mary Kate. The townspeople have all been shown to be waving cheerfully to Will and Tillane as well as metonymically to Sean and Mary Kate, so no one has suffered through the course of the film. Instead of ending on the culmination and success of Sean's marriage, the story ends with that marriage's completion and a new engagement, producing a sort of overdetermined and happy sexual state.

It is indeed difficult to speak about events and characters without considering their staging or narration. After this brief account of story resolution, we can now return to the textual discourse's closure operations and devices as evidence of how the ending really functions for the spectator. Discussion of story is frustrating since the linear, continuous story-line does such an efficient job of resolving itself. By looking at closure, however, and specifically the narrative voice, temporal and spatial ordering, and point of view structures, we can reconsider the textual functions of a Closed Text and find its true specificity, which is the binding-in of an active, unified spectator while simultaneously closing off the discourse patterns. In order to understand this double process better, we need to look carefully at the signifying practice of the text's narrative discourse.

Discursive Closure and Bracketing

A beginning consideration of the narrative discourse's closure should involve the largest structures and conventionalized strategies of how a Closed Text brackets itself off from a potentially endless fictional world. *The Quiet Man* is not as rigidly framed as some films, since neither the opening title shot of a small boat, nor the opening shot of the train, reappear at the film's end. Yet other discursive patterns do help bracket this film, signalling that strong ordering principles and a controlling narrative voice are hard at work. All three central theme songs, "Galway Bay," "The Wild Colonial Boy," and "Young May Moon," as well as the excited transition music (the "tiddly-dum" theme played for Sean's odyssey across the countryside, and other scenes), are played in a prelude under the titles and into the first sequence at the train station. These musical themes alternate throughout the film and return during the final scenes (30 and 31). Framing by musical theme is a recurring structure in the classical cinema, acting to enhance stylistically the controlled and predetermined activity of the film's narration. As Claudia Gorbman writes, "Musical recapitulation and closure reinforces the film's narrative and formal closure."[23]

Music acts as a closure device and is often essential, since its generally non-diegetic nature is meant to cover the final scene as it emphasizes or accents the visual action, while it marks the termination.

Earlier in *The Quiet Man*, this same technique appears when the musical volume is boosted, overtly signalling a change or culmination in action with the music track. During the fight sequence, the bass drums pound when Sean is hit by Will, and the fight theme music thunders abruptly when we see and hear Father Lonergan learning about the fight, even though he is fishing in a quiet stream, far from the battle. Earlier in the film there was a similar burst of music when Sean was struck down by Will at the wedding; the music thus serves as a shock by simulating the pain to Sean as he is knocked back to his memory of that repressed fight scene where he killed a man in the ring. Overt music used for an immediate expressive effect, coupled with its pacing and subdued thematic relations throughout the film, guide the spectator's attention and emotions while helping produce a soundtrack that is clearly marked as an enunciatory influence. For a secure closure, the musical chains must be closed off to end their own progression, as well as to act as closure devices to prepare the spectator for the text's last action: the closed ending.

The positioning of a reprise at the film's ending acts as a musical closure device tying together musical progressions, themes, and movements so that the soundtrack fits conventional structures of narration by closing itself off as a sort of autonomous musical mini-text. The music functions as a coherent, internally logical, and structured system that can begin and end on its own, while simultaneously paralleling the film's story. As a result, ending the music at the same time as other textual strategies doubles the impact of closure for both the music and the film. By ending several signifying systems at the same time, the film's termination point is strongly reinforced. By considering "The Wild Colonial Boy," we can see how efficient one of *The Quiet Man*'s musical motifs becomes as a discursive force:

> There was a wild colonial boy
> Jack Duggan was his name.
> He was born and bred in Ireland
> in a town called Castle Main.
> He was his father's only son
> his mother's pride and joy.
> And dearly did his parents love
> this wild colonial boy.
>
> At the early age of 16 years
> he left his native home.

And to Australia's sunny shores
he was inclined to roam.
He robbed a wealthy squireen
all arms he did destroy.
A terror to Australia was
this wild colonial boy.

The first introduction to "The Wild Colonial Boy" comes as a purely instrumental theme within the opening overture; it is set up as a traditional theme piece, reinforcing Irish connotations with its soft sentimental melody. But the full impact of the song begins to gain momentum when it is used diegetically in Cohan's Bar. After Sean has purchased White O'Morn, his first step in regaining his homeland, he offers a drink to everyone and explains his family lineage. The accordion player has been playing "The Wild Colonial Boy" very softly ever since Sean came in, but now, with the Old Man's acceptance of a drink from Sean, all the men in the bar sing the song along with, and in honor of, Sean. Everyone, including Sean, knows the words; the song thus acts as a unifying force to tie Sean to the local men, but that bond will be threatened by Will's blustery entry into the bar.

The song's third connotation, which builds on the first two meanings of its traditional Irish value, and its unifying function, is produced by its actual content, as the words comment upon both the action in the bar and in the film as a whole. The song is about Jack Duggan, a man "born and bred in Ireland," who returns home a hero. Thus, the lyrics encourage the spectator to equate Jack Duggan with Sean. While the song's hero went to Australia instead of America, Michaleen mentions to everyone that Sean's grandfather (Sean's namesake), "and a grand man he was, was hung in Australia." Sean's arrival in Innisfree is made even more mythical by this song, since the entire environment, right down to the songs the people sing, is constructed around a hero figure: Sean is the prodigal son Ireland has been waiting for. The paralleling of the *two* Sean Thorntons and Jack Duggan sets up *this* Sean as already Irish (he too is born and bred here) and something of an outlaw (though an accident, Sean did kill a man); thus the film's challenge is to work out Sean's progress toward being accepted as the Irish native that the song already acknowledges.

After this revelation of the "Colonial Boy's" lyrics, the song's traditional aspect, coupled with the local men's rendition to honor Sean, establishes a strong connotation of "Irishness" whenever the tune is introduced later. The fact that it is sung in Cohan's Bar also underlines the bar's importance as one of the first important cultural rituals that Sean must successfully pass through. Whether the melody is non-diegetically orchestrated or diegetically played on the accordion, it always serves as an element of both the story and discourse in its inscription of Sean as a returning Irish native and potential hero.

The final use of "The Wild Colonial Boy" illustrates its multiple significance as a device of both resolution and closure. When Will and Sean return home after their fight they sing "Colonial Boy" together. The fact that Will now joins in on the same song he had earlier interrupted illustrates that his acceptance of Sean is complete. Moreover, the song is here coupled with drunkenness, whereas Sean and Will's initial conflicts all arose over drinking arrangements in the bar. The fact that Sean sings along reiterates that he also sees himself as the mythical Jack Duggan. His victory in the fight, which wins respect from both Mary Kate and Will, ends his quest for Irishness and concludes his courting of Innisfree.

The tune "Wild Colonial Boy" becomes a closure device, wrapping up its accumulated significance and verifying the opening overture's use of the song. Thus it becomes a central musical motif and is thereby worthy of having been included in the beginning since it repeats and builds itself into an internal musical code in *The Quiet Man*'s larger soundtrack systems. The development and closure of one musical chain coupled with the accumulation and closure of the three other major musical themes, begins to show the music as a strong discursive structure that must be brought to its own closure to help secure the ending of the text as a whole.

All the signifying systems in a Closed Text lead up to the point where they conclude their own development in order to help close all the patterns of signification into an efficiently condensed ending. The musical overture in *The Quiet Man* overtly frames the soundtrack by opening and closing with a set group of themes that have accumulated specific meanings and effects throughout the text. As a result, musical closure is doubly active: first, it is a bracketing agent for the text, and second, it becomes a recurring element within the development of both the story and discourse.

Voice-over Narration as a Closure Device

The voice-over in *The Quiet Man* works to bracket the text, packaging it within a network of narrative voices, all working in unison to open, tell, and conclude the film. By the third shot of the film there are already two different narrative voices and points of view busy at work. Using Genette's model,[24] we can analyze voice and point of view by isolating four categories of narration:

	Internal Analysis of events	Outside Observation of events
Narrator as a character in the story	1. Main character tells own story.	2. Minor character tells main character's story.
Narrator is not a character in the story	4. Analytic or Omniscient author tells the story.	3. Author tells story as an observer.

In discussing the largest level of *point of view*, we need only analyze a film in terms of this chart's vertical (internal vs. external) demarcation, while the horizontal categories of the identity or status of the narrator help determine the kind of *voice* narrating at that moment.

It is not unusual for classical films to shift categories of narration; for instance a film like *Double Indemnity* (Wilder, 1944) begins and ends with an analytical, external narrator, or category 4, while the bulk of the story is told to us by protagonist Walter Neff, which fits category 1. *The Quiet Man*, however, is a bit unconventional in that the first few images of Sean's train arriving in Innisfree and the overture of non-diegetic music make the film resemble a normal omnisciently narrated situation (4). But when Father Lonergan begins to speak there is reason to question the film's internal narrator. Another thing to keep in mind regarding *The Quiet Man* is that the filmic "present" is very difficult to determine due to Lonergan's vague status as both character and ex-tradiegetic narrator.

In shot 4 Sean arrives at the train station and Lonergan's voice, which is as yet unidentified as that of a diegetic character, "begins at the beginning," in a forced Irish accent. This voice pushes the narrator toward a position as observer, or mode 3, since he seems to have access only to hindsight. Lonergan says of Sean, "He didn't have the look of an American tourist at all. Not a camera on him. What was worse, not even a fishing rod." This casual, comic narrator is obviously limited in what he knew of Sean, not even mentioning Sean's name, so that we experience the arrival as would a local witness (or at least as a fishing fanatic like Lonergan), and we are cued to wonder, like the villagers, why Sean does not look like a tourist.

This mysterious narrator's voice disappears as Sean's arrival unfolds, and the rest of the scene resembles a sequence typical of omniscient analytical narration. The shots following Lonergan's intervention do not look different than the several that preceded it. For instance, since there has been no switch to a subjective camera position, the opening images must be interpreted retrospectively as the vision of the narrating Lonergan. Otherwise, there must be several narrating forces working together. Throughout the film there is an opposition between the timeless, spaceless origin of Lonergan's voice, and the omniscient, linear unravelling of the story events. In fact the close-miking of Lonergan's intervention as voice-over narrator does not give any cue that he will ever exist diegetically within the world he is describing.

After the initial Lonergan narration, *The Quiet Man* advances from the seventh shot of the film to scene 4, shot 40, without the need for any further voice-over narration. The spectator has learned in the interim who Sean is and roughly why he has returned to Innisfree all without the aid of Lonergan. The presence of the Lonergan narrator has been so weak in fact, that it is nearly erased during this time; thus, when it returns during shot 40, the voice-over is surprising. At this point the voice-over finally justifies its presence and reveals its source. Lonergan's second intervention continues to pretend that the entire narrative is his handiwork: "Now then . . . here comes myself. That's me there walking, that tall saintly-looking man—Peter Lonergan, Parish Priest." Lonergan has had little narrative function so far besides commenting on events we can see for ourselves. The essential story elements have already been acquired without him; hence, instead of the narrative explaining why we are being told this story, or when it took place, we are introduced into it as if its importance were already understood. While the audience is not yet certain of Lonergan's specific narrative function or power, this folksy narration encourages both our mythical viewing of Sean's story and our anticipation of a comical narration of the upcoming events.

Immediately after Lonergan points himself out to the audience, Michaleen greets him visually and verbally. In effect, the information we received from Lonergan's voice-over is simply repeated in the diegesis. Why then does the discourse need the Lonergan narration and why is he so essential to the story? This move of the narrating voice from outside to inside the story, while keeping the point of view external to the main character, signals the audience to watch for a carefully structured narrative system. Moreover, the dynamic, comic character-narrator adds a new level of intimacy to the story. The text nonetheless seems to have an excessive narrating voice: The optical point of view is clearly that of a conventional omniscient narration (reinforced by the high-angle long shot to introduce Lonergan, rather than any strict point of view shot), and again, the story events seem to unfold without the need or constant presence of this voice-over narrator.

Lonergan's value and trustworthiness are immediately thrown in doubt as it becomes clear that in spite of his "Now then, here comes myself," the story is told *after the fact*. In this scene, Lonergan has to be introduced to Sean by Michaleen, proving that the Father Lonergan character of shot 40 has obviously not yet seen or heard any of the film up to this point. The time of narration is thus discontinuous since the spectators know more than Father Lonergan as character, but Lonergan's presence as a narrating voice implies knowledge and a narrating time scheme that are necessarily anterior to the fictional events. Hence, while the spectators know more than Lonergan the character, they also know less than Lonergan the narrator. Precisely what can be learned from Lonergan the narrator, however, is still not clear at this point in the film any more than the discursive time scheme.

When Father Lonergan makes his third major intervention out of the seven scenes in which he narrates, his position as a narrator is much more conventional. This time he gives the spectator information that would not otherwise be available: he tells who Widow Tillane is and then provides a background to upcoming events. All the while Lonergan continues to use a vaguely uncertain past tense. It is in scene 13, when Lonergan narrates over the images of Sean riding wildly across the countryside, that the time period is further confused: "Ah, those were the bad days. Sean with a face as dark as the black hunter he rode. . . . We knew things couldn't go on this way. . . . So we formed a little conspiracy. . . . And on the day of the Innisfree races we sprung a trap on Red Will Danaher." This narration, unlike Lonergan's earlier voice-over, covers the entire scene of Sean riding and being watched by others. Lonergan's narration has thereby accomplished what it had not yet attempted: it introduces the next scene, comments upon the events, and seemingly orders them for us.

It is this scene involving Lonergan's description of the thoughts and actions of the townspeople that seems to be the real narrative motivation for his presence as interdiegetic narrator. He is a voice in some later, nearly present time, spinning a fable-like yarn involving the frustrated lover riding like a black hunter, a popular conspiracy involving both reverend and priest, a cultural ritual in the form of a daring race, and a trap for "Red Will." However the real interest in this scene comes in its setting up of the last narrating role for Lonergan, the epilogue, scene 31.

The epilogue follows Will and Sean's entrance into the White O'Morn cottage. In this final scene, Lonergan's voice-over returns to mark the close of the discourse, thereby fulfilling the narrator's bracketing function. At the beginning of the concluding scene, shot 747, Lonergan begins speaking conclusively in a voice-over that suggests a termination point is approaching: "Well then, so peace and quiet came once again to Innisfree. We were. . . . Good heavens, what's that woman up to? Make way! She'll be running you down with that juggernaut!" The peaceful shot of a nearly empty street in 747 is followed by shot 748 of Mrs. Playfair racing her tandem bicycle out to the waiting crowd on the bridge. What makes this transition all the more troubling is that Father Lonergan is revealed present among the crowd, in shot 749, preparing to cheer Will and Tillane's courtship.

In these three shots the text has moved from imminent closure in the form of a concluding comment by Lonergan and a static end image of Innisfree, to a reopening of actions, underlined by Lonergan's own question, "What's that woman up to?" Between these two shots, the time and function of Lonergan's narration has again been complicated. In shot 747, he is concluding the tale of Sean, Mary Kate, and the town, speaking in a strongly marked past tense, but his narrating moment is interrupted as he shifts to the present and warns other characters to "make way." In both shots he is close-miked, implying a narrative never-never land, yet when he is shown among the townspeople, the audience must wonder where the narrating voice is coming from. Then, in shot 750, Lonergan climbs up on the bridge ledge to instruct the crowd in how to prepare for Rev. Playfair's arrival. Yet, here his voice fits the diegetic environment rather than being close-miked as in the voice-over.

The only satisfactory solution is that there are two Father Lonergans, at least in the way they function in the text: one is a character who is limited like all the others by the story's time and space; the second is a limited external character-narrator who knows more than Lonergan the character, but less than the film's primary narrator. There is a superior narrator who can interrupt Lonergan's narration, proving

Lonergan is not all-powerful or he would not have begun concluding the text before Mrs. Playfair made her entrance.

Primary Narrator and Epilogue

These seemingly contradictory functions between the character-narrator, and the larger narrative discourse as a whole, challenge the definition and operation of terms like narrator and discourse. Moreover, *The Quiet Man* forces us to distinguish carefully between various levels, degrees, and functions within the film's narrative discourse. André Gaudreault writes that the voice of a personified narrator, "is watched over by another voice . . . the voice of the fundamental narrator always dwells in the same transparent medium of the narration. It is the voice of the simple scribe of the diegesis."[25] Gaudreault's supra-diegetic narrator, like Genette's primary narrator, would seem always to be in power in any homogeneous text. However, in *The Quiet Man*, this superior voice is especially important since Father Lonergan is able to speak in voice-over, yet he rarely seems to *narrate* events.

The epilogue's revelation of the problems of Lonergan's narration mirrors his first two narrative moments when he described Sean's arrival at Castletown, but first met Sean forty shots later. In the epilogue, however, the time periods are doubly contradictory since the narrating voice's present time period takes place within the end of the diegetic time, which has already been set up as the past. At the same time that Lonergan the narrator says peace came to Innisfree, we see Lonergan on the bridge involved in a resolving event—preparing for Will and Widow Tillane to pass in Michaleen's courting wagon.

Lonergan's narration had been retrospective until shot 748, where his voice "distance" changes and he apparently speaks directly to fictional characters around him. This narrative shift from Lonergan's attempted conclusion to his shouting warnings to the characters, ends Lonergan's role as narrator and forces him to serve only as a character from this point on. He has nothing left to narrate since the fictional events have now overtaken the time of his narration. The discourse is back in the hands of the primary narrator who supplied the first few shots of the film. Thus there is a return to Genette's third category, the external narrator as observer, and the text has returned to a present tense in both its story and narration.

The implication of this confused temporal shift is that we would not have been told about Will and Tillane's engagement if Lonergan's narration had not been interrupted. For Father Lonergan, the tale told involved Sean's arrival in Ireland, Sean's difficulties fitting into society and marrying Mary Kate, and finally Sean's acceptance into the Dana-her clan. The termination point of this string of events would be the resolution of Sean's quest for his homeland, which culminated in his victory over Will, and the resulting "peace" after the fight. Similarly, the closure of this series of events would have been, and nearly was, Lonergan's wrap-up of the story. For a tight textual termination, how-ever, the spectator must leave the film with no cardinal story events unresolved; thus a new event, Mrs. Playfair's interruption, literally forces the text to continue until all actions are finished.

In this epilogue, the Rev. Playfair is guaranteed his continued position as parish minister, while Will and Sarah Tillane share Micha-leen's courting cart. Without this ending the spectator would be de-prived the pleasure of seeing the widow, who was the brunt of the trap against Will, rewarded for her kindness toward Sean early in the film. Lonergan's aborted first ending, "And peace and quiet . . ." would still have produced a moderately closed ending even without the resolution of these two plot points, but a higher degree of resolution results with these two final events following Sean's success.

Because Sean's happiness was so interwoven with other characters' goals, the minor plot lines, or unfinished story events of Rev. Playfair's security (ensured by his winning the bet with the bishop) and the Widow's future, would have been erased and nearly forgotten. Lon-ergan's closing narration would have been a relatively strong closure device at that point. The potential termination point achieved when Lonergan begins his final narration is therefore frustrated by this con-tinuing action, hence the second ending must be justified by strength-ening the scene's closure even further. In order to warrant this second conclusion, *The Quiet Man* makes use of one of the most secure closure devices available to the Closed Text film.

Once the Rev. Playfair has passed the crowd, there are several shots of Will and Tillane in the wagon, as Michaleen says, "No patty fingers if you please. The proprieties at all times." Suddenly the absurdity of the traditional Irish ritual is revealed: Michaleen's words recall all the problems that have been caused by following those proprieties through-out the film (and his statement refers back to his same role as referee and rule-maker at the fight during which Will refused to follow the boxing rules). At the end, however, the social traditions are still observed in spite of their flaws, proving the community is still intact. This return to stasis allows (and is allowed by) a secure Hollywood happy ending. Michaleen has returned to his role as matchmaker, Father Lonergan is still community leader, and the two largest landowners are about to be united in marriage. Most important, all these significant events reinforce the resolution of Sean's odyssey home.

Although the text was close to a termination point just before Mrs. Playfair interrupted Lonergan's speech, the second ending must secure the narrative discourse and sum up additional story events. The actual closure involves a rather conventional musical finale, but it also uses a theatrical foregrounding of the narration process itself by posing all the major characters for a closing curtain call. This last series of shots is represented as still within the diegetic space of Innisfree, though not the specific space in which the people were all last seen. In effect, the primary narration is now reassembling all the characters for our final observation.

Once Michaleen, in long shot, has driven off-right with Will and the Widow, there is a low angle, medium close-up of Fathers Paul and Lonergan pulling off their collars. This final action locks Lonergan into his observing character role (see fig. 2.13). Next, in shot 762, Mrs. Playfair and the young IRA man, look and wave off-right, then the shot series is anchored by shot 763, in which the train engineer, the mother-figure and the station master all look down into the camera and smile, followed by 764 with the old general and Feeney looking off-right. Next, shot 765 presents the three other train men looking off-right, followed by the old man (risen Lazarus-like) in 766, raising his cane, yelling and looking right into the camera (see fig. 2.14). Finally, in 767 there is a low-angle shot of Sean and Mary Kate looking off-right and waving (see fig. 2.15).

The time and space of this sequence begins at Michaleen's courting cart, a space Lonergan, Paul and Mrs. Playfair have all been instrumental in setting up. But suddenly there are shots of minor characters, staged side by side, facing the camera, though generally looking off-right and waving. The fictional recipients of these collective gazes and salutes would be Will and Widow Tillane, but the effect is of the characters waving at some unseen other—the narratee-spectator. Since these people are no longer posed on the bridge, the viewer must interpret their presence here as excessive, meaning it is not motivated by the same realistic or compositional logic as the rest of the film. The time and space surrounding these frontally-posed characters defies the continuous temporal and spatial codes for the rest of the film.

Fig. 2.13. Fathers Paul and Lonergan at the end

Fig. 2.14. Old fellow celebrates the ending

Fig. 2.15. Mary Kate and Sean wave back

The attention of these characters culminates in the final shot of the film, when Sean and Mary Kate, at home in the rose garden, also wave to someone off-screen. They are now included within the circle of looking and waving, even though this home space was previously treated as very private and isolated—the place where they discuss raising roses instead of children, for example. The backyard of the cottage was never established spatially as being visible by anyone else, even though the front of the cottage is shown to be visible from the Danaher property. Thus there is no way either to confirm or deny that Michaleen is driving past White O'Morn. Rather than being clearly functional, this final syntagma of everyone waving works conceptually to give the impression that everyone in Innisfree is celebrating Will and the widow's future together, while more immediately, it acknowledges the end of the narrative.

The third function of this sequence is to insert Sean and Mary Kate into the community so that by the time they are shown in shot 767, Will and the widow have nearly been forgotten because there are no inserted point/object shots of the wagon. Instead, the spectator can view Sean and Mary Kate's cheerful waving as a returning of the community's cheers—Sean and Mary Kate are waving back at the whole village, not just Will. Hence, Mary Kate and Sean become recipients of all other characters' salutes. A further effect of this final series of shots is to address the spectator. While the characters are apparently still in some Innisfree-looking location, they have left the logical time-space of the bridge, so their presence and gestures deliberately mark the discourse. The characters are not quite as theatrical as a play's curtain call, yet while they may not be standing in front of lights or cameras, they are positioned in a way never before seen in this film.

These characters may be cheering to Michaleen's courting cart on the level of story function, and to Sean and Mary Kate's union on a connotative level, but they are also addressing the spectator on a discursive level. The audience is implicated by the glance of these actors, and our presence as authorized voyeurs is openly acknowledged. Part of *The Quiet Man*'s narrational strategy has been to tell us a tale, complete with a folksy narrator, which has been underlined as pleasurable. This ending, to a large extent, has been able to carry that pleasure to its discursive climax when the entire cast celebrates the telling and resolution of the fictional events.

When Mary Kate whispers into Sean's ear, pulls away the ever-present stick, and leads him merrily back to the cabin, the music (bells and bagpipes now added to the traditional theme) joins in the celebration of their sexual union and the closure of the tale. The narrative has tied together all loose ends, and, on a global level, has just said "We have now finished telling you the story: didn't you have a good time?" The termination point is complete in that the fictional world's logic has been threatened by the direct address to the camera, hence Innisfree itself cannot be returned to. The film opened with a train's arrival and Sean's entry into Innisfree; it ends with a cart's departure, and Sean's entry into a cottage, a community, and a myth.

Point of View Structures in *The Quiet Man*

Intertwined with the role of narrative voice as it narrates and closes a discourse is the active production of a film's point of view structures. Point of view is essential to the narrating voice, the spatial and temporal narration of a diegesis, and the spectator's activity. However, it is also essential to a text's discursive closure. There are two kinds of narrative point of view in *The Quiet Man*: First, the largest level involves range of story information, or which characters have the most knowledge and see the most in the film; second, within specific scenes, perceptual point of view systems control the discursive structure.

Father Lonergan would be expected to have a central, organizing, even enunciating power as the character-narrator of *The Quiet Man*. Yet we have seen that his role as narrator raises more questions than it answers. For Lonergan to be able to narrate the entire film's events would require constructing situations *outside* the film to account for his knowledge of all the events for which he is not present. After all, Lonergan never seems to be near the action he is narrating. He is not at the train station to meet Sean, he is never in Sean and Mary Kate's cabin, he misses Sean's dragging of Mary Kate across the countryside, and he is late to the fight. Unless Lonergan has learned all of the film's events from the confessional, or in Cohan's Bar, (scenes never alluded to), he would have no way of knowing enough to narrate a story about anything, except perhaps trout fishing.

Michaleen Flynn is more mystical in being at the right place at the right time. He is at the train, he played with Sean as a boy, he is sitting outside the cottage window the morning after Mary Kate has fled, and he is also the only character to hum one of the film's theme songs. Yet there are scenes that even Michaleen cannot see, such as when Sean and Mary Kate escape his courting cart and kiss in the rain. No single character, not even Sean, has access to all the information of the film—Sean never even knows why he is supposed to take the Widow's bonnet at the horse race. Thus *The Quiet Man* becomes a film about what Sean *does* rather than what he *knows*.

The character points of view are all parts of a larger network and are controlled by an omniscient external narrator who can see into Sean and Mary Kate's private lives, but nevertheless chooses not to reveal some things to the viewer. This manipulative primary narrator gives Lonergan a weak but functional voice while itself maintaining story and discourse control. Hence, the conclusion wraps up the story and the ties off the narration from the unified, consistent primary narrator's point of view. The primary narrator's point of view is also present in the second, micro-level of point of view. Within specific scenes the excessive markings of an omniscient and omnipotent narrator are visible. This level helps insure both resolution and closure by the permeating spectacle of its presence. If the Closed Text is what Roland Barthes would call a "readerly" text rather than the more productively troubling "writerly," this is partly because its primary narrator is efficient at keeping the spectator entertained by its mastery, and comfortable by its maintenance of control.[26] The audience knows what the narrator wants them to know, and this is perceived as sufficient knowledge. The nar-

Fig. 2.16. Sean sees Mary Kate for the first time

Fig. 2.17. Mary Kate returns Sean's glance

Fig. 2.18. Mary Kate sees Sean's bed delivered

ration binds all the facts into a circle where everything necessarily fits; it is a narrative based on a principle of non-contradictions.[27]

The Quiet Man's narrator marks its presence clearly and playfully as both informed and informing. The first time Sean and Mary Kate see one another, in scene 4, shots 54 and 58, there is a low cut-in close-up on each of them, even though they are a hundred feet apart (see figs. 2.16 and 2.17). A low close-up of Sean smoking his cigarette, looking off left, is followed by a low angle close-up of Mary Kate looking right (with her mouth hanging open in surprise), yet this is not an exchange of points of view since the angle, distance, and line of perception do not fit either character's position. It is as if the narrator has taken the viewer right under their chins to witness the mythical meeting of Mary Kate Danaher and Sean Thornton. Such overt signals are a mainstay of classical narration; Virginia Wright Wexman finds a similar device used by D. W. Griffith in *Way Down East* (1920) where "David is clearly marked as the figure who will merge with Anna" as unmotivated close-ups idealize the couple early on.[28]

Throughout the film, the exchange of important glances becomes codified and differs in staging from other point of view instances. For example, another important exchange occurs during the arrival of the bed in scene 10. Here, Mary Kate is again shown in low angle close-up with her mouth open in amazement. Mary Kate watches the bed being delivered several hundred feet away, yet she is shot from very close range (see fig. 2.18). Sean and the Playfairs are much closer to the bed, but they are all filmed in medium shots. Mary Kate's glance is underlined as excessive and the style thereby signals that it is unusually significant that she stare in wonder at Sean's bed.

By the time the epilogue arrives, the spectator is cued that the intrusive narrator is again breaking up the space to emphasize particular character reactions and specific events. The optical point of view stays with the narrator: this final epilogue is no one's vision but is clearly orchestrated by the primary narrator. By the end, the object of the people's gaze has been lost or minimized since it has never been revealed to the spectator. These characters are more functional in how the audience sees them than in how they see other characters. If there is a glance exchanged in the epilogue it is a metaphorical one between the fictional characters and the viewing spectators rather than between the characters and Michaleen's courting cart.

A homogeneous voice has operated throughout *The Quiet Man*, even stealing away the internal narrator's visionary role, and as André Gardies writes, the classical narrative film reduces cinema's semiotic multiplicity by privileging the image over the actual sound-image interdependency, "producing a hierarchy of which the image is the primary beneficiary."[29] Since the audience has been taught to privilege the image, Lonergan's occasional voice-over is not interpreted as the controlling voice when compared to the primary narrator who is more evident in the selection of shot composition, editing, and musical intervention. The narration of *The Quiet Man* reinstates a unified narrative voice by the film's conclusion and, like all Closed Text films, the ending permanently reinforces the very selection of narrative events.

By the last shots of the epilogue the immediate story event of a new courting is exceeded and the last image, of Sean and Mary Kate returning the glances of the other characters, plays itself out. There is no return to a diegetic setting and no returned look from Will and the Widow. Instead, the spectator is left watching Sean and Mary Kate recede into the distance (mirroring Sean's arrival in the opening), as the music crescendos, while bagpipes join the theme. The audience is left with a resolved story and a concluded discourse, thus we now share the finished narrator's information and perspective. While the audience may ostensibly ask questions about these characters' futures, there is no textual demand that they ask anything beyond what has been presented. If the narrator has been trustworthy, thorough, and entertaining throughout the film, the ending is also pleasureable in that it resolves and closes the text, letting the narrative truly end rather than simply stop.

The Quiet Man and Closed Text Endings

As we have seen, the strict codification of closure devices, the repetition of obsessive glances, the progression of musical themes, and the control of the narration's voice and spectator's point of view, build together to make a very organized and tightly structured discourse. According to Colin MacCabe, "In the classical film the resolution of the narrative and positioning of discourses and spectator is re-marked by a very overt, often schematic plot resolution in which the restoration of an equilibrium is signalled on many codic levels (thus producing that effect of harmony—almost in a musical sense—so characteristic of the classical text)."[30] MacCabe's musical analogy is hardly random and fits the type of metaphor used by critics as diverse as Jean Mitry and Raymond Bellour, both of whom compare the classical film to a rhyming musical structure with its own sense of rhythm and its own internally consistent systems of logic or cause and effect. In films like *The Quiet Man*, a specific cause-and-effect action is created that fits the rules of Christian Metz's Plausible, which claims that a film may be unique on some levels yet still adhere to basic rules of classical cinema. In classical Hollywood cinema, specifically, the Plausible is determined by industrial restrictions and generic conventions. Once Sean Thornton has accomplished certain actions early in *The Quiet Man*, he is continually bound to those behavioral qualities. Similarly, on the level of discourse, the classical film must adhere to its own rules of acceptability and logic to produce a unified and plausible narration of the story.

The "happy ending" has become a cliché of the classical Hollywood cinema. It is often the goal of Hollywood stories to delight the spectator with the film's conclusion, rewarding the worthy protagonist and satisfying the desires of the audience by reinstating a secure and "proper" final situation. The conventions of the happy ending, like those for generic endings, have fit Metz's theory that the commercial cinema strives to be a *bon objet*, or the good object that the audience desires over and over. If the spectator can know the story resolution will be pleasureable as well as organically and causally rewarding, the cinema becomes a machine for enticing and then satisfying the audience. Metz writes that the industry, like an individual's own mechanisms of perception, works to reward the spontaneous desires to go to the cinema: One goes to the cinema because one wishes to and because one hopes the cinema will be perpetually pleasing.[31] The cinema guarantees its own continued existence as an apparatus of satisfied desire.

Added to the psychological seduction of the audience by the happy ending is the Hollywood cinema's use of a highly codified arsenal of discursive tactics to tell these happy tales. Bordwell writes, "Within the terms of Hollywood's own discourse, whether the happy ending succeeds depends on whether it is adequately motivated. The classical Hollywood cinema demands a narrative unity derived from cause and effect. . . . The happy ending, then, is defensible if it conforms to canons of construction."[32] Thus, in the Hollywood film the truly happy ending should be so logically generated by its telling that it does not appear to follow arbitrary conventions.

There are, however, Hollywood films that use very unmotivated happy ends that remind the spectator that the film must fit generic codes and that as a spectator they actually expect happy endings. In Sirk's *All that Heaven Allows* (1955), for instance, Cary (Jane Wyman) returns to Ron (Rock Hudson) only after she is told that he is injured and needs her support. The ironic addition of an unwarranted happy ending foregrounds the rules and restrictions of both the classical melodrama and audience expectations. In such films there is often a moment of displeasure or apprehension when the viewer believes that there will be an unhappy ending. When the potential for a "disappointing" ending is suddenly followed by an unexpected and tacked-on happy epilogue, which was unmotivated by either the story or its telling, the ending serves a double function of satisfying any desires in the audience for a happy resolution, while revealing the unnatural conventions of this and all fiction films.

In other words, an otherwise classical narrative can partially unmask the apparatus of the "good object" cinema by suddenly and unexpectedly attaching an obviously arbitrary end. A Closed Text film can thereby move toward being a more radical and open film. The disruptive value of such films as *Suspicion* (Hitchcock, 1941), *A Woman in the Window* (Lang, 1944), and *The Wrong Man* (Hitchcock, 1956) has been noted by Bordwell who writes, "It may be more provocative for the film to end happily than unhappily if the happy ending flaunts the disparity between what we ask of art and what we know of social life."[33] These films, like the more recent *sex, lies, and videotape* (Soderburgh, 1989), do not just make the real world more palatable by unwarranted cathartic endings, rather they foreground the artifice of narrative films and call attention to what spectators expect, or are thought to expect, from the cinema.

A classical film strives to make the obligatory reunion of the couple feel so correctly motivated—seeming to be the only logical ending—that the fact that the audience was already aware of the ending, or range of plausible endings, before entering the theater may be forgotten or repressed. A well constructed Closed Text builds toward an ending whose resolution and closure cover the marks of production, plausibly serving its generic guidelines, while simultaneously revelling in and repressing the arbitrary restrictions imposed by a classical happy ending.

Conclusions

In addition to strict generic or commercial restrictions, there are other structures that impose story and discourse logic onto a Hollywood film. Ideological structures also help determine plausible or "appropriate" endings in the cinema. For instance, Annette Kuhn refers to Mary Beth Haralovich's analysis of the women's roles in Warner films of the 1930s and 40s: "Haralovich has concluded that narrative closure is always dependent on the resolution of enigmas centring on heterosexual courtship: 'If a woman is in a non-normative role in economic control and production, she will cede that control to a man by the end of the film. . . . The courtship process itself constitutes a structuring element of their narratives.'"[34]

The Quiet Man fits this ideological, patriarchal structure, which is similar to the "taming of the shrew" motif in many Hollywood films—A happy ending here requires that Mary Kate Danaher is systematically humiliated by both Sean and Will before she can be "rewarded" with her husband, her furniture, and her garden. Ending with marriage in a classical narrative goes beyond mere story logic. As Rick Altman argues, while marriage is "that beyond which there is no more," it acts as a conventional termination point. "It arrests discourse and projects narrative into an undifferentiated 'happily ever after'. The comic equivalent of apocalypse, marriage represents a timeless, formless state in American mythology, precisely so that it will not be open to question."[35] Marriage thereby acts as an ideological end point, the restriction of woman, and the end of feminine "spunk" and independence, guaranteeing the desiring male's success.

Notions of closure involve industrial, generic, and ideological structures, as well as other dependent structures such as a star system. For instance, Jean Gabin had it written into his contract that he had to die at the end of his late 30s films, while Cary Grant could not play a murderer in *Suspicion*. The kinds of stories being told, and the manner of their telling, must be more closely analyzed for their internal and external systems of logic and conventional constraints before one can fully understand how endings motivate and generate a film's beginnings and middles.

CHAPTER 3

THE OPEN STORY FILM

My film [*The 400 Blows*] could end on neither an
optimistic nor a pessimistic note. I avoided solving the
problem. . . . Instead I took advantage of widescreen and
froze the image of my hero.
—François Truffaut[1]

The next three categories account for the wide variety of films that avoid
the finality of the doubly concluding Closed Text. Open Story films
involve a *narrative discourse* that is just as finished as in Closed Text films,
but their *stories* are left partially unresolved and thus significantly incomplete. While each of our subsequent three ending categories—Open
Story, Open Discourse, and Open Text—challenge classical norms on
some level, the Open Story film is the least radical since it typically
suspends the story before all diegetic events are finished, but it does
reinforce narrational closure. John Gerlach discusses literary texts that
fit this second narrative category: "The reader must often deal with the
open story, the story that seems to extend beyond the endpoint."[2] The
Open Story film stands as one lively alternative to the Closed Text's
secure buckling of resolution and closure, and as this chapter will dem-
onstrate, these films often motivate and justify their failure to resolve
by appealing to a realistic aesthetic.

An Open Story film makes a virtue of narrative strategies that would
cause problems for a Closed Text film like *The Quiet Man*. Here, if there
is a central character on a quest, the goal is never quite reached. In less
classical art film norms, for instance, there may be a cluster of characters
or one protagonist who will never achieve anything definite. Open Story

films thus lack any tight "tying together" of the minor satellite plots, while major ellipses abound that fragment, withhold, or even eliminate story events. While some critics fault such films as unfinished, defenders of Open Story films are quick to compare the openness, irresolution, and weakened unity of action in these films as honest avoidance of artificial story norms and a celebration of ambiguity in art and the real world.

Critics as different as André Bazin, Frank Kermode, and Pauline Kael praise fiction that preserves a sense of contingency, since chance and uncertainty permeate our experience in the real world. Gerlach also supports complexity and openness as more "natural" storytelling traits: "The issue was not that narrative falsified our view of the world but that causal chains were far more complex and subtle than direct linear patterns of fiction."[3] Films with open stories too are often interpreted as striving for a new, less conventional, more vibrant relation with real experience; thus the Open Story film breaks away from the more codified reality of the Closed Text. Consider Pauline Kael on François Truffaut's work: "The meaning of these films is that these fortuitous encounters illuminate something about our lives in a way that the old neat plots don't."[4] Armine Kotin Mortimer, writing on novelistic closure, is equally pertinent when she claims that in light of André Gide's work, modern novelists must grope with asking "How can one pretend verisimilitude . . . without encoding a lack of finality? . . . How does one render an unfinished life in a finite form?"[5] Open Story films satisfy viewers looking for accessible alternatives to formulaic classical form; hence critics often valorize or even exaggerate the diegetic "purity" created in these more naturalist inspired films.

Open Story films generally pursue more engaging ways of signifying a somehow more honest or immediate fictional world. In fact, films with an inconclusive termination often raise problems that the author or narration present as unsolvable. For instance, Italian neorealists and their followers are quick to underline the virtues of stories that lack conventional resolution: The audience cannot say where Francesco is at the end of *Open City* (Rossellini, 1945), or whether he will return to orphaned Marcello (see fig. 3.1), nor how Antonio Ricci and his son Bruno will survive in *The Bicycle Thief* (De Sica, 1948), nor what eventually happened to any of the characters still alive at the end of *Paisan* (Rossellini, 1946). André Bazin, writing on Vittorio de Sica and Roberto Rossellini, sums up this faith in loose story construction and narrative irresolution: "The empty gaps, the white spaces, the parts of the event

Fig. 3.1. *Open City*. Francesco says good-bye to
Marcello

that are not given, are themselves of a concrete nature: stones which are missing from the building. It is the same in life: we do not know everything that happens to others."[6]

The lack of happy or even definitive endings is one of the qualities stressed with regard to the neorealists, and this same absence was certainly a strategy expanded upon by many post-World War II art films. As Kristin Thompson writes, "From the late 1940s on . . . ambiguity as a cue for realism became a familiar convention. Italian Neorealist films like *The Bicycle Thief*, with their open endings and chance events, were among the first films to draw on this notion extensively."[7] She also points out that the realism attributed to de Sica's film "lies in those areas where they depart most from classical usage. Its subject matter draws upon an historically recurring notion that a concentration on the working and peasant classes makes for more realistic action. The narrative based on this subject matter then introduces a considerable number of peripheral events and coincidences.[8] The films in France of Robert Bresson, Jacques Tati, and the French New Wave, are also among the important sources for an aesthetic of openness.

77

Obviously, however, there have always been open-ended narratives and not all Open Story films depend upon realistic motivations for suspending the action. For instance, some films play with notions of subjectivity that are left ambiguous at the end. For instance, Fellini's *8 1/2* (1963), Verhoeven's *Total Recall* (1990), and *Jacob's Ladder* (Lyne, 1990) all begin with mental subjective images but end with scenes that cannot be easily recouped by the viewer. Is Guido's final round-up of all *8 1/2*'s characters in a circus ring a metaphor? a dream? or the film he eventually shoots? Similarly it is not clear whether Quaid is really on Mars or dreaming a fantasy vacation at the end of *Total Recall*, or whether Jacob in *Jacob's Ladder* is hallucinating again or "really" dead. Even Ridley Scott's *Blade Runner* (1982) preserves a certain irresolution since the film suggests blade runner Deckerd (Harrison Ford) may suspect that he too is a replicant, but the dreamlike happy ending never confronts that option. Such endings rely less on a drive toward the ambiguity of real life and instead revel in the playful uncertainty of their own narrative worlds.

As we expand on our study of kinds and degrees of story openness, we should keep the following question in mind: How are the ends of films like de Sica's *The Bicycle Thief* with Ricci and Bruno walking off into the crowd, or Truffaut's *The 400 Blows* (1959), with Antoine Doinel standing alone on the beach, any more open and unresolved than *Shane* (Stevens, 1953), with its hero's lonely ride into the sunset? The goal of this chapter is to reveal, by looking in detail at *The 400 Blows*, how analyzing a film's story development and conclusion clearly and productively differentiate the viewer's role in reconstructing the stories of Antoine Doinel and Antonio Ricci from those of Shane or Sean Thornton.

Truffaut's *The 400 Blows* serves as a good bridge between the phenomenological past of Jean Vigo, Jean Renoir, and the neorealists, and subsequent trends of modern European cinema. The French New Wave as a whole serves as an excellent example of a wide range of storytelling options, and *The 400 Blows* fits well into the Open Story aesthetic of suspended story construction. As David Bordwell and Kristin Thompson write, New Wave narratives build on loose causal connections: "Moreover, the films lack goal-oriented protagonists. The heroes may drift aimlessly, engage in actions on the spur of the moment."[9] The story of Antoine Doinel, like that of other New Wave characters, from Chabrol's *Cousins* (1959), to Paul in *Masculin-Feminin* (Godard, 1965) or Jerome in *Claire's Knee* (Rohmer, 1969), is much more elliptical than classically unified and conclusive tales. As Allen Thiher writes, the episodic nature of *The 400 Blows* springs from Antoine's own fortuitous choices, making Antoine Doinel "something of a prototype of the existentialist hero."[10] *The 400 Blows* in particular also became celebrated for providing just the sort of irresolution that satisfied both modernism and New Wave demands for openness; as Anne Gillain writes, each of Truffaut's films attack the problems of narrativity and closure from a fresh perspective, and *The 400 Blows* may be seen as a model for all Truffaut's subsequent work in these areas.[11]

A second motivation behind working on *The 400 Blows* is that the film became the first in a series of Antoine Doinel films. Every film series involves some degree of continuation from one film to the next, yet most such films are simply Closed Text films that follow one another rather than leaving key chains of events suspended at the end. Typical film sequels, like *Charlie Chan in Egypt* (King, 1935), use a repetitious cycle of closed stories with the main characters returning to act out similar events in each episode; the Doinel series[12] functions quite differently. This distinction between the Doinel series and Closed Text sequels like Charlie Chan, *The Thin Man* series, or James Bond films, is best explained in light of Gérard Genette's theorization of continuations. He writes that a sequel often exploits a work's success, prolonging its story, while "a continuation does not necessarily complete the *immediate* story of its hypotext, so it may pick up the tale many years later."[13] Similarly, while *Return of the Thin Man* prolongs the story of Nick Charles, as he and Nora take the train home from their first episode, Truffaut's continuing "biography" of Doinel supplies more tales from Antoine's life with *Love at Twenty* (1962), *Stolen Kisses* (1968), *Bed and Board* (1970), *Love on the Run* (1978), without really filling in the gaps from the end of one to the beginning of the next.

The Antoine Doinel series was also erratic in its production (the films were not regularly produced, no one ever knew when the next one might appear), and the series followed the Léaud character through a life cycle as he grew, learned, and repeated some of the same mistakes while aging realistically. Only with Truffaut's death in 1984 did the series really end. The Doinel continuation then, unlike the *Thin Man* serials, did prolong "slice of life" representations of a character's life without ever summing that life up. The conventional serial film resolves and then reopens, while the Open Story film is inscribed from the beginning as full of gaps that are never resolved. The Open Story spectator is warned that not everything can be known—not just because it is being saved for the next episode, but because the Open Story's aesthetic strategy celebrates the uncertainty of knowledge and the contingency and incompleteness of real life.

Open Story films, however, are not perpetual-motion narratives either. While the stories of *Open City* or *The 400 Blows* are not fully resolved, their narrative discourses are closed. Unlike a soap opera that continues indefinitely and, as Robert Allen claims, "lacks a 'form' in the traditional sense,"[14] Open Story films do have termination devices to tightly close their narration. One of the tasks of this chapter, therefore, is to study the interrelation between discursive structures that manage to retain ambiguity and contingency in the stories while maintaining a conclusive network of discursive systems.

Story Irresolution and Action Codes in *The 400 Blows*

Truffaut's *The 400 Blows* grows out of *Cahiers du Cinéma*'s early New Wave period (an era of pastiches and homages dedicated to Louis Lumière, Renoir, and Rossellini, among others), that resulted in such diverse films as Louis Malle's *The Lovers*, Truffaut's *Les Mistons* (1958) and Jean-Luc Godard's *A Bout de souffle* (1960). Many of the early New Wave films, like the neorealist films that preceded them, could serve as examples of the Open Story category, since they relax the constraints of the more unified, symmetrical cause-effect ordering of the classical cinema. Truffaut proves a good test case since his earliest films satisfy Open Story traits and are often interpreted as realistic on some level: "The swift changes of mood and pace that characterize his films are an attempt to match his form more nearly to the way life usually develops. We don't live life according to 'genres.' Nor is life . . . a taut unbroken chain of significant acts, linked by logic, as it is sometimes made to appear according to the editing pattern and plot development of the traditional cinema. Indeed plot often disappears, as it virtually does in *The 400 Blows*."[15]

As we analyze how Open Story films are constructed, how they function, and finally how they can be identified and analyzed, it is important to begin by studying their unresolved story since that is the Open Story's distinguishing feature. During this discussion it is again necessary to refer to a detailed shot-by-shot decoupage (see Appendix B). This analysis was made from the original Dyaliscope print and contains 404 shots.[16]

As we saw earlier, a story is perceived and understood by the spectator as a series of interrelated functions, indices, informants, and characters, each of which has a varying effect on the micro-level resolutions within individual scenes and on the ending. Only by studying the degree of resolution within the actions (after witnessing the action x, do we experience its effects on other actions?), the events (does a given situation develop, stay the same, or only suggest it may change?), and character (do the characters progress toward any new functions, or remain static?), can we understand and assess the overall extent and function of story irresolution.

It is best to begin by summarizing the final scene of *The 400 Blows*. This final scene, like that of *The Quiet Man*, does contain some returning motifs and some completion of story events begun earlier. However, instead of *completing* earlier action codes, these events merely refer to and continue them. In *The 400 Blows'* final sequence, 19, Antoine escapes during a soccer game and runs to the sea; once there, however, he turns back toward the shore (and the audience) only to be stopped in a freeze frame. Within this last segment we can isolate important cardinal story functions, and find definite hinge points where the plot offers two or more options from which the characters may choose. Nonetheless, these story elements will not resolve their accompanying chains of action and events, instead they will only continue them.

We need then to consider the events of segment 19 as they relate to the major action codes of the story as a whole. The sequence follows a dissolve from segment 18. In that scene, Mrs. Doinel visits Antoine at the reform school and tells Antoine that his father is now disinterested in his fate (shots 394 and 395), and that Antoine will be apprenticed out to work after he leaves the Observation Centre: "You wanted to earn your living, now you'll see if that is any fun." Shot 396, the end of the scene, shows Antoine in close-up, isolated in a dark space looking sad as the image slowly dissolves into segment 19, a long shot of the boys marching off to the soccer field (see fig. 3.2).

This final scene begins with Antoine in a more serious and solitary situation than ever before. If there is to be a resolution in the classical sense, Antoine must accept or reject his situation; he is at one of Barthes's cardinal function points. At this place in the story the spectator is left with a number of central questions: How will Antoine deal with his parents' rejection of him? Will he wait out his time in reform school, then take a job? Or will he fight against that single option? Don Allen's psychoanalytic character reading of Antoine interprets Mrs. Doinel's breaking of all bonds with Antoine as a personal trauma for Antoine, as an end to their Oedipal drama, and as the forceful removal of the

Fig. 3.2. *The 400 Blows.* Boys at Observation Centre marched to soccer field

forbidden object of his desire. For Allen, "Antoine's behavior pattern when faced with a crisis remains consistent: he runs away. At the end of *Les Quatre cents coups* he is free at last—and utterly alone."[17]

Allen's character analysis does provide one possible option for understanding the contradictory nature of this final segment, which admittedly resolves a plot point of the previous segment, since he escapes rather than obey the school/job option. Yet this sort of resolved action works only on small event-to-event levels. It does not complete the development of either Antoine's character or the events that have been developing. Anne Gillain also pushes the Oedipal struggle to extremes in interpreting *The 400 Blows.* For her, Paris is the "maternal space" Antoine must move away from as he passes from the imaginary to the symbolic stage of development. This opposition allows Gillain to claim that the ending is not an incomplete action but the achievement of a rebirth.[18] Antoine's escape does decide one option, and whether this does or does not fit psychoanalytic models of an Oedipal journey's completion, in terms of the manifest story the escape is *not* complete; rather than accomplishing a narrow escape to freedom like that of Rosenthal and Marechal in *La grande Illusion* (Renoir, 1937), Antoine

82

never finishes escaping. In *The 400 Blows*, we do not know whether Antoine is only five minutes ahead of his captors, whether he has eluded them, or what will happen in one-half hour of story-time after our last shot of him. This lack of completion on the large story level is one of the charms of the Open Story film, and of *The 400 Blows* in particular, since small, event-to-event and segment-to-segment chains can keep starting up and finishing throughout the story but the largest codes remain open to speculation.

Before accepting any claim that Antoine is free at the end of *The 400 Blows*, however, one must look more closely at the story events of segment 19. The first of the film's last seven shots recalls the other, more playful gym class when Antoine and René (like the boys in Vigo's *Zéro de conduite*, 1933), had broken away from their oblivious instructor while jogging through the streets of Paris. While that first escape was joyfully innocent, the second "outing" has the camera shooting the boys straight-on instead of from a high angle, and they are now escorted on either side by the guard-instructors. This shot is both a contrast to the earlier gym class and a confining image after Antoine's frustrating conversation with his mother. He is being coldly marched toward a new but grim destiny devoid of any free play.

The somber piano score in this sequence contrasts sharply with the optimistic accompaniment of the earlier gym scene (segment 10), and the penny whistle recalls the teacher's whistle in the other scene. The gym teacher's whistle returns throughout the game scene, but the whistle changes functions from setting a cadence as it has in both jogging scenes, to regulating the soccer game, to acting finally as a police whistle when the teachers chase the fleeing Antoine. In this way the earlier Vigo-homage-joke of the gym class is transformed into a more serious situation of gym teachers acting as police agents trying to capture the escaping Antoine. Earlier, Antoine had avoided the running exercise, while here he sets a fast pace, eluding the sport teachers. This sort of turn of the tables rhymes the initial jogging scene and provides one mark of a controlling, scripted narration.

Conventional interpretations of *The 400 Blows* include attempts to make the end more resolved and complete than the story warrants. The English class in segment 9, during which Mrs. Doinel comes to get Antoine after his night spent away from home, includes the repetition of the phrase "Where is the father?" The question obviously relates to Antoine's illegitimacy but also to his eventual escape after his mother's news that Mr. Doinel is disinterested in Antoine's fate. Thus,

Antoine can be seen as having lost still another father, and this loss triggers his escape. Antoine is orphaned and left to the reform school; as long as he is cut-off from family and friends, he rebels against the new authority and flees. But this sort of reading simplifies his character and assumes a conventional cause-effect which *The 400 Blows* struggles against.

During the same English lesson, the second exercise asks "Where is the girl?" Unlike the father question, this one has a definite answer: the girl is at the beach. This scene is seminal in that it works with the mother's later plea to the judge asking him to place Antoine in a detention center near the sea because Antoine has never seen the ocean. In this way Antoine's escaping to the sea looks like a preplanned story move, resolving at least the minor goal of Antoine visiting the ocean. The "visit," however, is highly ironic: rather than vacationing, he is running away so the sea becomes a barrier more than a destination. While Antoine had mentioned earlier that he wanted to join the Navy, he cannot yet go onto the ocean, so he only looks at it, gets his feet wet, and then turns away. Reaching the sea is both an accomplishment and a new failure since the ocean offers neither respite nor response to his plight.

Like many critics, Georges Sadoul overemphasizes Antoine's final act, as if his running to the sea completed the film as a whole or anchored its global meaning. In writing about René and Antoine, he claims that while "Swiping things here and there, they dream of going to the ocean. To get money for the trip, the boy takes a typewriter."[19] But René and Antoine never mention needing money to see the ocean, when they do find money it is for immediate pleasure: they go to the amusement park or the cinema. In shot 238 of scene 13, Antoine mentions the ocean, but the Navy is still his only hope of getting there. René, on the other hand, has seen the Channel and ocean already and never shows a desire to go anywhere. Interpreting the end as an ironic conclusion to the boys' desires and plans, or believing that Antoine's trip to the sea has motivated the theft, minimizes the contingency of the film's events and ignores Antoine's more immediate needs in sequence 13, namely food and shelter.

If Antoine can be said to have a goal as a character it is to be accepted by the adult world. Acceptance for Antoine would involve his teacher's praise and understanding for his love of Balzac, whose work is far superior to the banal rabbit poems and grammar repetitions the teacher offers in class. It would also require that Mr. Doinel take a stronger interest in Antoine's life. (When Antoine mentions the rabbit poem Mr. Doinel thinks he is referring to the nursery rhyme of the tortoise and the hare, further underestimating Antoine's age and intellect.)

Obviously, however, Antoine's largest and most important desire is to be wanted by his mother. Mrs. Doinel, as Antoine tells the psychologist, was not only unmarried when she conceived Antoine, but also wanted an abortion (see fig. 3.3). Antoine's knowledge of these facts, coupled with his disgust with her for taking lovers, makes impossible the happy reconciliation of son and mother. Thus, one possible resolution point that is suggested by the themes of this loosely plotted film, but rejected by the ending, would be the achievement of a definite conclusion of the mother-son conflicts.

Instead of a film that moves toward any such thematic resolution, *The 400 Blows* is a film constructed out of seemingly chance events that complicate rather than complete such thematic developments. Antoine's story is composed of brief vignettes which generally end in some incomplete manner, as in the case of Antoine's looking for diversion in the amusement rides only to stumble upon Mrs. Doinel kissing another man in the streets (see figs. 3.4, 3.5, 3.6). This event advances the plot but is never resolved between the boy and his mother. Furthermore,

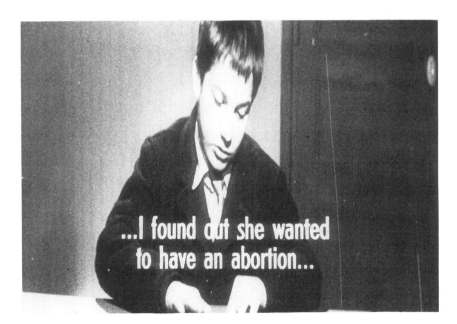

Fig. 3.3. Psychologist's office

Fig. 3.4. Antoine in the rotor amusement ride

Fig. 3.5. Antoine sees his mother kissing a strange man

Fig. 3.6. Mrs. Doinel sees Antoine

Antoine's search for satisfaction is not at all defined and when he does have a short-term goal, such as achieving a high mark on his French composition, it ends in disaster and opens more problems than it solves. As Karel Reisz and Gavin Millar write, "Antoine's life is described not so much by a series of dramatic events as by a string of nonevents: roaming the streets, playing truant, visiting the fairground, mooning about the flat . . ."[20]

Searching for tight cause-effect relationships between the story events allows an interesting perspective into the construction of Open Story films. Looking for a single goal, as in Sadoul concluding that Antoine seeks a glimpse of the ocean, helps, paradoxically, show the gaps in the story rather than supplying a termination point. The effect of contingency in the ordering of events and the seemingly haphazard linking of the film's actions, eventually works to decrease any expectation of homogeneous event-to-event repetitions. For instance, during *The 400 Blows*' third scene Antoine forgets to buy flour, Mr. Doinel buys a fog lamp for the car in preparation for an automobile club outing, Mrs. Doinel shows her disgust toward her cousin's repeated pregnancies, and Antoine takes the garbage down. None of these acts ever develop in the film, so they are offered as representative events rather than the basis for any future scenes: Antoine's forgetfulness will be seen again when he forgets the burning candle, but the flour episode was hardly necessary for understanding that later event. In *The Quiet Man*, Sean mentioned how he would honk his car horn when calling on a woman back home, which in turn prepares the later scene when he honks the new carriage horn to cue Mary Kate to run outside. In *The 400 Blows*, however, there is never any such subsequent significance to the auto club (Antoine does not steal car parts, the father never has an accident in the fog), Antoine's forgetfulness is never important for the plot, we never meet the pregnant cousin, and Antoine never falls down the stairs while taking out the garbage. (It is not difficult to imagine a Hollywood version of this film in which the family would be reunited by some unexpected tragedy such as Antoine's falling down the stairs or being struck by the father's car.) The events flow without causal motivation even though tangentially they enrich characterization. This free-flowing story pattern keeps the spectator from expecting a unifying or culminating denouement. In fact, the more the story employs such loosely connected scenes and irresolution on the micro-level (like "Why do Antoine and René take some little girl to the puppet show?") (see fig. 3.7), the less likely it is that the viewer will *expect* a tight completion of events by the end.

The Open Story film, unlike more classical texts, does not allow a termination effect to put the film as a whole into a compact thematic structure. Critics like Sadoul, Allen, and Gillain may try to interpret the ending of *The 400 Blows* as the motivated escape to the sea, or the final liberation of Antoine from his Oedipal attachment to his mother, but their explanations are threatened by the film's resistance to encapsulation under a single, dominant, containing theme. Thus, a film like *The 400 Blows* presents the difficulty of resolution right from the start by never presenting the story of Antoine as the simple progression toward any final completion point.

For a moment then it is important to turn to the notion of thematic progression in the story of *The 400 Blows*. Don Allen writes that there is a central, dominant theme to the film which is "that freedom is inextricably linked with isolation."[21] As mentioned, however, it seems questionable to interpret Antoine's escape to the sea as achieving any real freedom. By contrast, Fontaine of Bresson's *A Man Escapes* wins an ambiguous but tangible freedom via his physical escape. Antoine, however, is not so free since there is no final image that would signify completion of the escape. His escape came as much by chance as did his being punished for having the picture passed to him in the first scene of the film. By the end Antoine is shot in medium close-up so that the surrounding space is denied, as is any alternating syntagma to locate the pursuers. Antoine may be outside the reform school, but he is not represented as safe or free. Moreover, up until the end, Antoine usually escaped with René; thus while Antoine is certainly alone at the end, this resolution is not enough to make all earlier crises logical precursors. Antoine's first escape was a cheerful one, going to the movies and riding the rotor machine, while his last escape is his most important and most serious. Yet these two instances hardly build to a central theme of the loneliness of freedom.

The facts and events accumulate in Open Story films rather than build together toward a symmetrical resolution of actions and theme. This construction, reflected in the ends of *Paisan* and *Open City*, is provisional, almost arbitrary. *The 400 Blows* has a story that reaches a plateau and stops, yet it could have ended with Antoine sitting in the cage at the police station, or, as in the original script, later than it actually does, when Antoine returns to Paris (see fig. 3.8). As Sadoul writes, "There is neither a 'happy ending' nor an 'unhappy ending.' It is an 'open end' with a question mark . . . this story flows along like life."[22] *The 400 Blows*, with its twists, gaps, and asymmetry, does not prepare the audience for a specific happy or unhappy resolution, it simply stops when the telling concludes.

Truffaut, writing about Italian neorealist story construction, claimed that Rossellini had no set narrative pattern nor any structural problems in telling a story, since the point of departure simply determines what direction the story will follow: "Given any character, his religion, his eating habits, his nationality, his activities, he can only have certain needs, desires and certain possibilities of satisfying them." The conflict, according to Truffaut, will develop naturally, and "There is no longer any problem in ending the film: the finish will be dictated by the sum of all the elements of conflict."[23] Similarly, the end of *The 400 Blows*, with Antoine escaping from the reform school, does not tie off the story's conflicts, but only acts as a further example of them. There is no resolution of those conflicts, only their sum, or rather their accumulation.

One reason the Open Story film can so often be constructed along an accumulative narrative pattern (whereby adding or even cutting out whole sequences would not qualitatively change the plot of the film), is that it uses a less linear, more open action code. *The Quiet Man* was not resolved until Sean's marriage became a happy one and he was accepted by the Innisfree community, because the whole story construction

Fig. 3.7. Antoine and René take a girl to puppet show

Fig. 3.8. Antoine in the police cage

focused efficiently on the events which were crucial to Sean's success or failure. Films like *The 400 Blows* or *Paisan*, however, do not have such efficient and directed action codes. Instead, the films concentrate more on a series of scenes than on a continuity of actions that hook one into the next until the final event is achieved. By the middle of *The 400 Blows* we know many of Antoine's character traits, as well as some facets of his environment, but there is no single quest or goal in sight for him. There is not a special project brewing that can resolve Antoine's tensions in school and at home. In the end, the story only offers a cluster of events that add up to a life-style and a character, rather than any climactic resolution. In fact, as Bordwell writes, "At the close of *Les 400 coups*, the freeze-frame becomes the very figure of narrative irresolution."[24]

Narration and Point of View

In one of his early reviews of *The 400 Blows*, Jean-Luc Godard wrote that the film would be "the proudest . . . and the most liberated film in the world," being open in both its theme and its style.[25] But while the thematics do indeed remain open, the narrating level is not as free as its camera movement, widescreen composition, and long-takes might suggest. To be a truly "liberated" narrative discourse, the narrative voice would have to be more unstable or heterogeneous. Thus the exhilaration which so many people found at Truffaut's film may have been due to a break from the norms of scripted and efficient storytelling, but this alone hardly makes it a truly open text equivalent to Godard's own *Tout va bien* (1972) or *Weekend*.

In order to prove that *The 400 Blows* has a closed narrative discourse we must analyze its narrative voice. Because the presence or absence of a narrative voice is always a matter of degree—the narrator is always present—any analysis of narrating voice must ask just how absent the voice is throughout the text. The narrator of *The 400 Blows* is outside the action and outside the characters; thus it consistently maintains an extra-diegetic and hetero-diegetic presence.

The focalization of this narrator shifts a little, as it can in any text, but for the most part, the range of information allows Antoine only to be observed, never understood. The audience begins constructing Antoine's character out of glimpses of his actions and his conversations with René, but the narrator rarely allows us inside Antoine's mind. The absence of subjective information also helps weaken the "goal-oriented" nature of Antoine's progress through the story. The spectator can never be sure what Antoine wants, because the narrator does not become internally focalized around his thoughts; hence the resulting variety of thematic readings drawn from this film. The focalization does shift occasionally, but very briefly; for instance in sequence 11 (shot 213), Antoine, assigned to write an account of some serious personal event, recalls the Balzac novel he read in shots 208–210 (see fig. 3.9). In a subjective voice-off, Antoine repeats the final words of the novel, "Eureka, I've found it," and launches into re-writing the Balzac passage. There are only a few instances where the focalization changes; the rest of the time the narrator restricts the range of information to Antoine without expressing exactly what Antoine thinks.

The consistent narrator fits Jean-Paul Simon's "category II" of the four modes of enunciation in which the narrative voice mode is "I am absent" while the spectator's is "You are present." This is his category for classical fiction that may use multiple secondary identification systems such as a shift in focalization, but the story is nonetheless narrated by a unified individual voice that is reassembled in the spectator's imaginary.[26] Because of a text's reliance on a stable and unified narrating voice the spectator maintains a consistent relation to both the narration and the narrated systems of the film. The narrative voice in *The 400 Blows* is thereby able to create a diegetic world in which the spectator will marvel at the rotor ride, ponder those little girls in the cages at the reform school[27] (see fig. 3.10), and worry about Antoine left all alone and trapped on the beach. The narrative discourse thereby employs what Jacques Rivette called "an equality of voice" to guide the film and its spectator toward a pleasurable and constant identification with its fictional universe.[28] The *tranche-de-vie* story can only work with a convincing discursive system behind it.

In the film's final sequence the labor of this narrating discourse can be witnessed as it heightens and maintains the spectator's involvement and identification with the diegetic events of Antoine's escape. During the final sequence, 19, Antoine makes a break from the soccer game, which is presented in one long shot and then a medium shot. By shot 400 the camera is above the game, and on the outside of the fence. When Antoine throws the ball back in to the game, he runs left to the fence (see fig. 3.11). The camera follows him and tilts down slightly; then once Antoine has succeeded in slipping under the fence, it pans back to the whistle-blowing coach who then repeats Antoine's motion. The camera again follows the coach until it pans further left to show Antoine, now in long shot, running back into the frame (see fig. 3.12).

The camera was in the best position to follow Antoine's escape in a single take, yet since the long shot repeated the opening shot of the game (398), it appeared as chance that Antoine escaped right to the corner of our vantage point. In shot 401, the coach runs in a low-angle medium long shot to the right, then there is a tilt down revealing Antoine hiding under the bridge; Antoine is shown to the spectator just before he runs off left. The camera has for a second time shown itself to be tied to Antoine's actions without the viewer receiving any cue that the narrator was anticipating Antoine's movements. This camera work is surprising since the camera has so often simply followed Antoine, often seeming to have come across him by chance, as in the gym class or puppet show scenes. Now, in the final sequence, it anticipates his actions by knowing when and where Antoine will escape and what path he will take. This camera does not follow or show any other character now for the final three shots; most significantly, it does not reveal where the pursuing teachers are. Instead, the camera keeps itself, and the spectator, close to Antoine until the end.

By maintaining a final series of medium long shots and medium shots, the narrator begins to show its mastery, revealing its knowledge while at the same time intensifying the spectator's identification with Antoine. It is impossible for the viewer to make comparisons between the related positions of Antoine and the pursuers because there is no alternating syntagma to inform the audience fully. By tracking along with the running Antoine and passing meaningless road signs, the viewers are as lost as he. Because the audience does not know where Antoine is going, the result is an apprehension and concentration around him. Only when Antoine sees the ocean in shot 403 does the camera follow Antoine's glance and leave him to show the sea, but then Antoine runs into the shot, away from the camera and toward the beach. In the final shot (404), the camera is down on the beach, but its continued follow-pan to the right as Antoine trots toward the ocean covers the jump of camera location: Antoine looks to the sea, walks in the water, but then turns toward the camera and approaches it (see figs. 3.13, 3.14, 3.15). As he comes into medium close-up the frame freezes and there is an optically printed zoom into a close-up of his puzzled face.

The entire final half of sequence 19 has narrowed the spectator's information to be equal to Antoine's knowledge. Earlier in the film the spectator was allowed glimpses of events which, although related to

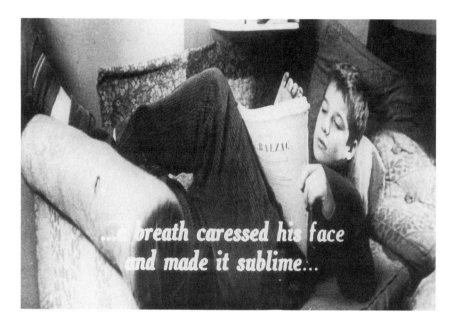

Fig. 3.9. Antoine reads Balzac

Fig. 3.10. Girls in Observation Centre cage

Fig. 3.11. Antoine runs from soccer match
(shot 400)

Fig. 3.12. Antoine chased by coach (shot 400)

Fig. 3.13. Antoine runs toward the sea (shot 404)

Fig. 3.14. Antoine turns back toward camera,
optical zoom begins (shot 404)

Fig. 3.15. Antoine in freeze-frame (shot 404)

Fig. 3.16. René leaves Observation Centre

Antoine, could not have been known by him. In sequence 4, for instance, the narrator reveals Antoine's classmate Mauricet spying on René and Antoine, while in scene 6 Mauricet is shown coming to the door to inquire after Antoine's health while Antoine is on his way to school. The spectator has heard Mr. and Mrs. Doinel read Antoine's farewell letter as well, and learned he misconjugated *comprendre*, to understand, while Antoine was simultaneously finding a place to sleep for the night. Even during the reform school scene the narration presents images and sounds that signal the gravity and sadness of Antoine's situation, yet he could not have had access to any of these elements. For example, the camera moves outside the walls to watch René pedal off while the soundtrack follows the conversation *inside* the school as Mrs. Doinel tells Antoine that his father did not come along to visit him (see fig. 3.16). Antoine's thoughts are with René as René rides off, yet his aural perspective places him inside with his mother.

While the narration of *The 400 Blows* occasionally provides us some events or actions denied Antoine, the final decision to limit the audience's perception to what Antoine sees is a strategy that helps close off the omniscient narrative discourse with an expressive containment of the narrative systems. By the end of the film the point of view is restricted to Antoine's actions. The audience knows even less than the fleeing Antoine at this point.

But how does all this narrowing of spectator knowledge and the intensification of the extra-diegetic distance between the narrator and the events affect a secure closure? By limiting the spectator's knowledge, the narration narrows the viewer's range of expectation. The audience is in no position to question the narrator's choices, only the narrated events themselves. This narrator maintains a strong control and reinforces the story's ambiguity, and eventually it finishes by imposing a very strong closure device—the freeze-frame of Antoine looking back at the shore and camera. The optical zoom finally erases the diegetic space-off, channelling Antoine's look into the camera and back to the spectator. As Arlene Croce has written, "At the end, you are no longer looking at the film—the film is looking at you."[29]

Antoine's glance, like the more optimistic wave from Sean and Mary Kate at the end of *The Quiet Man*, creates a narrative termination point, so this returned look, which has so far been one-directional, sets up a discursive end point. The final shot arrests the discourse, unveiling the narrator's control and terminating our passive voyeuristic relation to the film. As the film's subjects, the audience has always been in a privileged position, but the last four shots condense that observing place by confining and further directing the scope of our look until finally the viewers are in a position from which there is no return: the audience is "seen" by Antoine, and the audience sees most overtly the narrator's presence. Once the narration acknowledges the spectator and the camera, the fiction ends even though some of the story's action codes remain unresolved.

On the discursive level, the audience's look throughout *The 400 Blows* surrounds Antoine and only rarely leaves his side. Even when there is any jump to a space where Antoine is not present, the jump is to an event that relates directly to him. Antoine is the enounced hub of Paris for this film, and therefore he is also the only real object of visual fascination and attention. The final scene's progressively decreasing focalization begins paring down the role of Antoine so that now it is no longer the look of the other surrounding characters of teacher, parents, coaches or even psychologist that fix upon Antoine, but instead he becomes the place of the spectator's (and narrator's) glance alone.

As the single object of our collective gaze Antoine is made the nucleus of the film's space and the intersection between the three filmic glances of the narrator, characters, and spectator. By employing such a centripetal locus of space and glances, the film concludes when this object of fascination is made immobile. The last shot thus freezes more than the image; it also arrests the play of the glances that have surrounded him. This shift of the narration's attention toward the apparatus transforms Antoine from a solid body moving through space into a figure of the arrestation of the film's driving strategies. The "stilled" Antoine becomes an image of termination; the optical zoom approaches, turning him into a static spectacle. There is nowhere for the viewer's glance to wander. The point of view structure has changed the spectator's look into a fixed stare, freezing the action codes and closing the narrative discourse by giving a final, impossible view of Antoine.

Musical Score as Closure Device

As mentioned in the discussion of *The Quiet Man*, visual point of view is only one of many systems at work within narration. Classical soundtracks actively support the spectator's identification with the diegetic events. Jean Constantin's musical score for *The 400 Blows*, like

Victor Young's for *The Quiet Man*, has several melodies that cue specific moods for the film. The opening title sequence (shots 1–9), provides an overture of the film's most significant musical themes, running from the strings' sensitive melody to the slower piano music that is used later for instances of irony or danger (as in sequence 4 where Mauricet spies on the boys while they hide their books to skip school). In addition, the opening includes the slowest and saddest music (the plucking strings along with the oboe and xylophone solos), which later accompany Antoine to the police station.

The 400 Blows has a fairly limited set of musical themes upon which several variations are performed. The overture sets up an easily recognizable array of emotional music that directs and enhances the spectator's response to specific scenes. At the end of the film, sequence 19 begins with the cyclical chords of a piano playing the same tune usually plucked by the strings, a five-note round, joined by a penny whistle as the boys jog off to the soccer game. The music ends so that wild sounds of the soccer game can prepare the slow, quiet setting from which Antoine will escape. Then the only sound left is the shrill blowing of the guards' whistles. Other than these whistles, Antoine's escape is only accompanied by the diegetic sounds of his footsteps, heavy breathing, and dogs barking in the distance. This use of wild sound corresponds to what Claudia Gorbman defines as "diegetic silence."[30] Here, the absence of music helps focalize the spectator's attention onto Antoine's plight and reinforces his isolation. However, by the time of the tracking shot of Antoine running off right (shot 402), the music's final movement begins to reassemble all the film's melodic motifs.

This finale creates a musical wrap-up and epilogue. The strings slowly rise into their tragic medley and are joined by the xylophone and piano, recalling Antoine's ride in the paddy wagon. As the shot continues, Antoine sees the ocean, runs away from the camera, and a crescendo brings the full orchestra back to take over from the building piano music. At this point a bell tolls and the xylophone and flute dominate in order to direct the viewer's reactions since these two instruments were used often for the playful jazz score that accompanied René and Antoine's earlier romps through Paris. Next, the diegetic sound of waves begins to challenge the music for volume and dominance. The slow, serious repetition of waves takes over the rhythm as the orchestra drifts off, leaving only the plucking guitars that dwindle during the last half of the final shot. Finally, even the guitars diminish until one single guitar plucks out the theme song during the freeze-frame and continues, along with the sound of the waves, through the fade to black.

The musical themes begin as culturally coded motifs, calling upon pitch, rhythm, and melody to prepare the viewer for certain emotions, but they soon accumulate more specific, functional significance as the film progresses. Hearing a mournful piano theme or a cheerful jazz piece in the beginning, the spectator can anticipate the kind of scene that will follow, or at least the audience has a stock of emotions handy to go with the appropriate musical motifs. The music of *The 400 Blows* calls upon the spectator's knowledge and experience of other, pre-textual codes and contexts. Furthermore, by the film's conclusion, the jazz score has accompanied the gym class when Antoine and René evaded the instructor, as well as the time they addressed the priest as "Madame." The sad theme has also been associated with Antoine's arrest, so the concluding medley carries a double significance: First, it has its own emotional connotations that exist independent of the film, while second, it recalls the specific story events that accompanied it earlier. These musical allusions help the audience compare such scenes as Antoine sitting in the paddy wagon, or his wandering about alone and hungry, peeking in shop windows. Gorbman labels such strategies "cinematic musical codes" since much of the theme's final meaning is based on specific filmic context and is thereby "associated with a character, a place, a situation, or an emotion."[31] Since *The 400 Blows* has so few musical themes they become comparatively precise in denotation and connotation by the end.

During the title sequence, the music signals the range of emotions that will be addressed, but by the end it recalls the specific images and events already underlined by the music. As a result, the final medley not only brackets the film by ending the film musically as it had begun, but also calls forth the various connotations that have been established throughout the film. When Antoine runs alone in the final four shots of the film, the music replaces his thoughts, supplying us with a sort of condensed flashback to the film. The "happy" jazz score is now made tragic by its inclusion in the sadder dominant theme, so the music acts as a sound montage, calling upon references to the film's more significant events. The music makes the spectator remember key scenes, and hence it summarizes the film's emotional and connotative peaks like audio flash cards, ensuring a single interpretation to the rather ambiguous ending of *The 400 Blows*. The spectator may not be able to guess where Antoine is going or even whether he will get away, but everyone feels his loss and recognizes this musical strategy as the soundtrack's most conventional and secure closure device.

Strategies for Ending Open Story Films

While the bracketing strategies, so strong in the voice-over narration of *The Quiet Man*, are limited to the musical overture and reprise in *The 400 Blows*, the film still has a securely closed narrative discourse. One reason the bracketing is less evident in the Open Story films in general is that the weaker or more absent story resolution does not necessarily inscribe the cyclical or "bookend" discourse that a more closed story will demand. Tight story continuity aids in the use of appropriately repetitious and enclosing narrating strategies, less resolved stories generally lack the more obvious discursive closure devices and replace them with more subtle strategies. For instance, neorealism, which works upon strategies of objectivity and naturalistic causation, also contains many films that satisfy the requirements of the Open Story category. The endings of neorealist films such as *Paisan*, *Open City* or *La Terra Trema* (Visconti, 1947), all have strongly marked endings, yet they use devices that do not undercut the unresolved quality of the story events.

The restriction of the camera's mobility and point of view is often a common trait at the end of these films: The boys retreat slowly toward the city below in *Open City* (see fig. 3.17), Antonio Ricci and Bruno walk away from the camera as it cranes up in *The Bicycle Thief*, and Antonio sets out to sea once again at the close of *La Terra Trema*. This failure to follow the characters, unlike the overt salutation of films like *The Quiet Man*, *Band Wagon*, or even *Little Caesar*, works to allow the characters to continue on their never-ending paths while the camera, narrator, and audience are all left behind. The closing gesture of an Open Story film often acknowledges that while this stage of the tale is finished, there is never any resolution to the type of drama being told. These endings encourage readings of diegetic ambiguity. They also elicit the sort of observations made by critics like Sadoul, Roy Armes, and Annette Kuhn, that the open endings are somehow more life-like since their tales begin *in medias res* and conclude before a final, apocalyptic ending.

Robbe-Grillet, writing about slice-of-life narratives, argues that by the text's end the narrator will always give the impression of being able to furnish more information. Thus, even though the ending may seem

Fig. 3.17. *Open City*. Boys walk back into Rome

to complete the narration, the audience would have only been presented parts of the diegetic world; any complete image of the fictional world should remain beyond the grasp of narrator and audience alike. Moreover, these tales strive to suggest that had the audience asked the narrator for more information than was presented, the narrator could have complied; hence, the story material, like real life, could be continued indefinitely.[32]

Neorealists often create Open Story films that valorize their lack of story resolution as a more accurate portrayal of lifelike characters and situations. The typical neorealist film, however, like *The 400 Blows*, does not threaten the closure of the representational codes and systems of conventional cinema. Instead, the non-professional actors and location shooting still fit within very monological narrational strategies. Many critics recognize the loose narrative relations in neorealism. Bordwell and Thompson, for example, write that "The most formally innovative Neorealist films allow the intrusion of noncausally motivated details."[33] Thus the novelty and even formally radical nature of these films involve the insertion of details that do not seem essential for the given story or its dominant plotlines, but the narrational tactics themselves still provide discursive closure. One of the most lucid critics of neorealism is Rossellini himself. In an interview, Rossellini supports this notion that neorealist films emphasize the story elements over narration: "The realist film has the 'world' as its living object, not the telling of a story."[34] Rossellini's aesthetic preference leans toward texts that recreate a diegetic world situated between a real documentary representation and an imaginary one. His films set up a conventionally coded vision wherein the telling is efficient and appropriate for such contingent story events, yet the proposed problems lack any final resolution.

Neorealism is founded on an illusion of reality that may follow different codes of representation than the typical commercial cinema by using exteriors and non-professional actors. Yet the overall discursive pattern in neorealist films parallels that of a conventionally closed text. The story may be left unresolved, and thus earn praise from critics like Bazin, but it is important to note that the irresolution of major action codes continues in spite of the definitive closure of the narrative discourse. Thus, Antonio Ricci may continue his search for his bicycle, yet the film itself uses several closure devices to produce an Open Story narrative wherein the *told* is not resolved but the *telling* is concluded.

One other narrative strategy alluded to earlier, but not yet explained is the possibility that some Open Story films are composed along lines of paratactic ordering. Parataxis allows for the coherence of a narrative's themes to be independent of the sequential organization of the story elements. Use of paratactic ordering is common in folksongs and even myths where the rearrangement of story elements in their order of presentation does not damage or confuse the story. For example, switching verses three and five of a seven-verse paratactic song would not alter the theme or tale presented, since linear progression is not an essential component of these works.

There are also paratactic structures in narrative films. By discussing two such films, *Paisan* and *Mr. Hulot's Holiday* (1953), it is possible to see how paratactic ordering functions in some Open Story films. Paratactic texts do not lack a logic or order, but unlike more linear texts in which removing or rearranging sections will change the story and leave inconsistencies in the discourse, the paratactic text may be enriched or impoverished but not essentially altered. The ordering of story elements within these narratives includes events that usually follow one another either logically, temporally, or in accord with some principle of serial generation.[35] Ordering a film according to a system of days or seasons is a common paratactic strategy.

For example, other than a few accumulating gags in *Mr. Hulot's Holiday*, such as the falling taffy or the loud record player, there is no event that would be confused or weakened by switching what happens on the second and third days of Hulot's vacation. Kristin Thompson has also noted that the film's comic scenes "are not causally connected in linear fashion, so that many could be rearranged without affecting the basic minimal proairetic line."[36] Similarly, in *Paisan*, which is a collection of short Open Stories, there is no linear necessity other than the invasion route of the American soldiers that determines which stories occur in which order. There is a looseness allowed by the lack of a dominant hermeneutic code, or a central, goal-oriented character. In spite of Hulot's apparently making a date to go horseback riding, (which he never accomplishes), he is never shown as caring or planning to do one activity rather than another (which is certainly part of the film's satire on vacations); and the lack of any individual character being present in more than one of *Paisan*'s segments also allows the freely interchangeable units or mini-stories in that film. One structural challenge to a truly paratactic system is that, once set in motion, it may not possess an easily determined concluding point. How does a narrative that lacks a definite goal or resolving end point conclude? Most often some formal bracketing closure device is employed.

In a long poem of an *abab* rhyme scheme for instance, the shift to *aa* in the last two lines, or an *abc* final three lines, will act as a closure device by signalling a discursive change of strategy. Ending after an *ab* would merely stop the poem in mid-air, regardless of the content, while an appropriate closure device, which must be recognized as such by the reader, will conclude the poem. By opening and closing a poem with the same line or verse, by ending a novel with a scene parallel to the text's beginning, or by using music or other narrating systems to mirror the opening of a film, a conclusive discursive bracket can close a paratactic text. Another strategy for ending such texts, and one used by Tati in *Mr. Hulot's Holiday*, is to use the natural end point of the temporal series. The film is structured around the days of the week so it can end on the seventh day, the natural end of one week and the end of a vacation. Thus, while *Mr. Hulot's Holiday*'s middle section may indeed be paratactic, there is a discursive closure generated by the film's seven-day structure.

The sequential nature of a paratactic text implies continuation as its narrative principle, thus closure for such a text will be aided by some external, conventional intervention so that even a paratactic structure inscribes some termination point. A consistent, monological narrative voice will also aid in the closure: because there is a consistent rhythm to *Mr. Hulot's Holiday*, with the day/night/day fades and the use of the shutters as a discursive punctuation mark, the narration is in a good position to put an end to its own system. The paratactic text may appear to have a loose event-to-event narration, using each sequence as a "cellular unit," as Noel Burch writes, but a unified narrative voice guides the spectator to an inscribed and satisfactory termination point.[37]

An additional perspective that helps isolate Open Story films is to look at the move by more conventional films toward a new ambiguity of story and plot resolution. Annette Kuhn, writing about "New Hollywood Cinema," confronts closure in both the mathematical sense of containment and the open-ended sense. She writes that both *Julia* (Zinnemann, 1977) and *Girlfriends* (Weill, 1978) depart modestly from the classic realist model in their narrative resolutions. In each film the questions set up by the narrative are not fully answered. Instead, the result is an open ending that takes on a particularly feminist quality: "The women's relationships continue to be problematic and contradictory, yet important enough to be continued."[38]

This openness of theme and character relations is interpreted by Kuhn as a very positive force working against the tight and stereotypical resolution of so many Hollywood cinema films, wherein the problems raised by women within the fictional world are solved by marriage or death. An example of women being killed off in order to cease to be a problem for the narrative can be seen in the death of the Shirley MacLaine character, Jenny, in *Some Came Running* (Minnelli, 1958). In that film, Jenny dies just after marrying Dave Hirsch (Frank Sinatra); moreover, she stops a bullet meant for him. Her death allows Dave to have "done the right thing" by marrying her, while he is rewarded by the probable love of the more socially acceptable teacher, Miss French. Thus *Some Came Running* resolves the "woman problem" with marriage *and* death.

Kuhn's view of open-ended narratives fits an almost Bazinian notion of a spectator's active participation arising from the portrayal of a more open and realistic diegetic world. These ideas come close to the neorealist aesthetic which also boasted that they brought the spectator nearer to everyday perception of typical, unresolved, and even ambiguous events. The films preferred by Kuhn are not those fighting against discursive closure, or that foreground a new "feminist" discourse, since these films, like the work of Marguerite Duras and Chantal Akerman, fall into the trap of limiting their potential audience to film students and academic feminist viewing communities. Instead, she follows the Truffaut, Bazin, and neorealist schools in calling for films which engage broader discussion and participatory viewing.

The last consideration of the Open Story film involves the phenomenon of the film serial. The idea that many films may be generated from a single "source" film is important in the definition of the Open Story category. Clearly one of the narrative strategies of the serial involves presenting a number of individual episodes in order to continue a story and replicate a successful commercial venture. However, the fact that a series must by definition continue something, whether it be a string of Fantomas, James Bond, or Thin Man films, does not immediately qualify every serial film as an Open Story narrative.

Films like *The Empire Strikes Back* (Lucas, 1980) or *Dr. Mabuse the Gambler* (Lang, 1922), leave one narrative thread hanging or at least unresolved at the end of each episode. However, the fact that Hans Solo is taken away by the evil characters at the end of *The Empire Strikes Back*, or that Mabuse escapes in Lang's film, does not automatically imply that these films share the Open Story text's unresolved ending. These episodic films, like television soap opera formats, have continuing chains of action, some of which may be answered within the film (Mabuse loses the battle and his band of counterfeiters is crushed). Yet one additional action chain is either left unresolved or a new one is reopened in the closing minutes of these films. Mabuse has somehow escaped, and his escape, like the capture of Hans Solo, works as a hook to allow the possibility for a subsequent episode and the continuation of the series.

The audience expects a narrative thread to be left untied in series films, but the spectator also expects the episode to stand fairly independently; hence, the films are usually sold as both single product and as one episode in a continuing series. The film series involves a classical text film in most cases, with all major action codes completed (James Bond has triumphed, Mabuse's plot is foiled), but some new wrinkle is often left open at the end, assuring the audience that future episodes will finally resolve these issues. This strategy is similar to a television series that uses two-part episodes: the audience knows that Batman will not be killed in the next episode, but they are pleasantly disappointed by two-part episodes because the resolution is delayed "until next week" at a particularly suspenseful moment.

Some critics, especially in television studies, argue that the notion of a continuing series is somehow radical practice, or even a "feminist" strategy, since they lack conventional resolution. Television's need for continuous program product in order to guarantee a stable advertising incentive, however, is far different from the reasons for openness in an Open Story film. On the other hand, the TV series may not be very different from the marketing of the James Bond and Star Wars serials. To claim that *Dallas* or *Amos and Andy* is somehow "open" just because it continues for many episodes, however, would force us to consider *Star Wars* too as a radical departure from classical behavior. The notion of a continuing narrative has been around in many formats and genres and is certainly not new to literature, broadcast, or the twentieth century. Television, specifically, has several types of series and needs to be studied with reference to its own historically determined modes of narration.

Thus, what Robert Allen's careful analysis of soap operas proves is that the "protensive indeterminacy" of the continuing television or radio series allows a commercial option for indefinitely postponing the termination.[39] But what his study does not do is adequately test the degree of discursive closure and narrative irresolution in individual programs. In narrative terms, therefore, the fact that *As The World Turns* comes back every week may not be as important as the degree of closure and resolution that each particular show maintains. The pre-condition that a program will return tomorrow is one major difference between the television soap opera and the truly Open Story film; the former works by a system of extended action codes which do in fact end (someone does eventually decide to marry, divorce, or take the new job), but Open Story texts leave the actions suspended with no promise of a return to the characters or their dilemmas.

What this consideration of various series proves is that the simple existence of a chain of episodes does not mean that a specific film, or television show for that matter, is necessarily open. Instead, like novels written by Charles Dickens or P. G. Wodehouse, which were published chapter by chapter, the serial end is only delayed, protracted, or dis-placed, not left unresolved. There are also films that were not originally made with a sequel inscribed in their story, but instead their sequel was generated by financial strategies rather than narrative ones. At the end of *Jaws* (Spielberg, 1975), for instance, there is not even the Dr. Mabuse-like threat that the evil force may one day return, yet the film became the financial flagship of a series of Jaws movies.

Similarly, *Friday the 13th* (Cunningham, 1980), *The Thin Man* (Van Dyke, 1934), and *Star Wars* (Lucas, 1977), are all links in a chain of sequels, but that does not make them *a priori* Open Story tales. A film, whether unique or one of a series, must be analyzed closely before it can be judged as an Open Story narrative. The continual survival of James Bond is not sufficient to produce narrative irresolution. Instead, the major hermeneutic codes must be plotted to see whether they are in fact completed—opening a new question mark at the end of the film is not sufficient grounds to consider that story as a whole open. In practice, many of the serial films do reach a termination point, then simply open another action code to guarantee a continued audience by playing with audience expectations, but this does not necessarily lead to a narrative strategy of "ambiguity," since it may simply be a tactic providing simple narrative delay.

As we have seen, the Open Story film covers many kinds of cinematic practice and many of these films foreground their open stories as attempts to break away from the tired story forms that require a tight, parallel structure and strong resolution. The analysis of *The 400 Blows* has shown that in spite of these less goal-oriented characters, the seeming contingency (or even inefficiency) of the represented story events and the marked irresolution at the end, the narrative discourse remains unified, directed, and homogeneous, producing a conventional closure within the film's discursive structure. The loose story lines tend to open up the temporal and spatial relations between characters and events, so that, as Jacques Rivette wrote about *The 400 Blows*, the spectator is offered a film, "with a point of departure and an arrival point, while between them is a whole distance to be traveled."[40] Gone is the point-to-point economy of story symmetry that was so essential in the Closed Text films. With *The 400 Blows*, the story pretends to be more honest while it uses less conventional story logic. Both these tactics produce a story that cannot be resolved since a definite ending, be it happy or sad, would limit the diegetic world that was carefully presented as open and natural in its lack of typical story ploys.

It is not surprising, therefore, that the first noun Godard used to describe *The 400 Blows* should be "frankness,"[41] nor that this Truffaut film should fit the same category as most neorealist films. Because these films do represent a believable, vibrant diegetic world, and since Truffaut is influenced by Bazin and the neorealists (Rossellini was one of the first people to read the script), and since Renoir's films influenced both the neorealists and the New Wave, this category seems both historically justified and quite homogeneous in the kinds of films it includes.

The end result of the Open Story film is that it manages to create a conventional narrative discourse of a less complete story in order to get closer to everyday experience or to break formulaic notions of plotting. By discarding the stylized, rhyming, even repetitious story events of the Closed Text films, these films remain more open on the level of character, events, and actions, even though they do maintain a classical hierarchy of narration. The film ends, concluding in a secure systematic way, while the story is left unresolved and open with the possibility of continuation. In this representative Open Story film, Antoine is on the beach, but why and where he will go next is left permanently open.

CHAPTER 4

THE OPEN DISCOURSE FILM

Film theory is descriptive; it strives to account for observable phenomena in films and also, by creating formal models, to envision figures not yet realized in actual works.

—*Aesthetics of Film*[1]

A Theoretical Category

Within the grid of all possible relations of story to narrative discourse, I am proposing four possible types, yet the category of Open Discourse is markedly different from the other groups in that it is a more abstract and perhaps even "virtual" category. To begin with, an Open Discourse film has a resolved story, but an open narrative discourse. The films do not use any codified closure devices; hence no narrative termination effect is established. In this way, the Open Discourse film is a mirror-image reversal of the Open Story film, since one structure—here, the narrative discourse—is left open. The Open Discourse film, therefore, shares a resolved story with the Closed Text, but has a narrative discourse that is as inconclusive as that of the Open Text. However, as we are about to see, open discursive strategies undermine a story's ability to be resolved and the pertinent, organizing question for this entire chapter becomes, Can a story truly appear resolved to a viewer when the narrative discourse remains radically discontinuous, dialogical, and open?

The most interesting aspect of the Open Discourse category is that it suggests that narrative discourse can continue after the story is complete; it can exist without any "story" to tell. Yet our narrative model demands that a narrative have something to narrate, so narration in and of itself, would not seem to be able to exist without some story. Thus, in this Open Discourse category, the narrative discourse will have to continue narrating story elements that do not contribute in any way to the primary, already resolved, story. The narrative discourse in an Open Discourse text must then be excessive in that it narrates elements which do not continue the text's central story. Moreover, these elements must not simply present a new complete or appended story or undercut the achieved resolution, or the result will be open story and discourse: the Open Text film.

One of the problems in explaining the Open Discourse category is that there are no strict examples of fiction films that *fully* fit the category's requirements. There are films that help suggest what a truly Open Discourse film would be like, but so far none completely satisfies the third category's demands. The lack of a concrete film example, however, does not minimize my four-category scheme, nor does it allow us to withdraw the Open Discourse group from this project. On the contrary, the Open Discourse category becomes more vital to this study because it is the point at which the model's theoretical consistency is fully tested, while it also provides a productive look at why the other three categories are dominant in the narrative cinema. The Open Discourse group, therefore, becomes the location where both the present narrative model and the very definition of the narrative cinema itself are pushed to the limit.

It is important to justify the validity of establishing such a theoretical category before describing in more detail what an Open Discourse film must or must not do or citing films that approach these requirements. In any theoretical construct the system proposed must always be involved in a dialectic give-and-take between the theoretical concepts and the body of texts which do, in fact, exist. Any narrative analysis that attempts, as this book does, to divide various filmic texts into categories, groups, or genres, must constantly shift between the critical constructs on the one hand, and the materiality of the films on the other. The process involves beginning with the observation of specific films, constructing a proposed theoretical structure out of those films, and then constantly rechecking those hypotheses against additional individual films.

Tzvetan Todorov, in *The Fantastic*, outlines this very process and explains the duality of any critical study that tries to group individual texts into larger genres. He declares that the concept of "genre" may be defined to have two potential meanings:

> In order to avoid all ambiguity, we should posit, on the one hand, *historical genres*; on the other hand, *theoretical genres*. The first would result from an observation of literary reality; the second from a deduction of a theoretical order. . . . It is therefore necessary to deduce all the possible combinations from the categories chosen. We might even say that if one of these combinations had in fact never been manifested, we should describe it even more deliberately: just as in Mendeleev's system one could describe the properties of elements not yet discovered, similarly we shall describe here the properties of genres—and therefore of works—still to come.[2]

Todorov's position is crucial here since it describes the elementary interdependence between historical and theoretical genres; moreover, it simultaneously stresses the value of the purely theoretical category. In the present analysis of endings, the narrative model involving story and narrative discourse is based upon observation of individual films, yet that model suggests the existence of the Open Discourse film. It must be remembered that specific closure devices evolve within history, therefore the four categories of endings must protect this potential for change in the future while they recognize what has already evolved in the past. The logic of this third category rests upon both historical and theoretical analysis. As Todorov continues: "The definition of genres will therefore be a continual oscillation between the description of phenomena and abstract theory."[3] Thus, this category of the Open Discourse film should be seen as growing out of historical observation while simultaneously remaining essentially theoretical.

Story involves an interrelated series of events containing characters, actions, informants, and indices, each of which may affect the resolution of individual scenes, as well as the end of the film as a whole. Yet, as we saw with *The 400 Blows*, not all story elements work to further or accomplish a resolution of the story's action codes or complete its major story events. A Closed Text film like *The Quiet Man* may have all its story elements interwoven into the film so as to serve the final homogeneity of the story's action (the rose garden, the big stick, the courting wagon), but the Open Discourse film will have story elements (primarily informants and existents) that are present *after* the major actions, characters, and events have all combined into a resolution.

A film does need some story elements to narrate at every moment in the film, yet the degree to which the collection of existents and informants constitute a completion of the film will vary widely. In an Open Discourse film, therefore, the characters may reach their anticipated goal and all the related actions codes and story events may be completed, yet the film's narrative discourse continues. This final portion of the film, following the resolution of the overall story action, will involve some discursive strategy that does not reinforce or expand the resolution that has preceded it. A film may continue after the story is resolved, and it will necessarily include images and/or sounds, but the material used will not constitute a new complete story nor will it complete earlier action. In other words, not every collection of story elements or even dialogue will constitute part of the preceding story.

Here, story must be seen as double: on a general level, it is the narrated material, while on a second, cause-effect governed level, story is the arrangement of some of those elements into a directed, developing, and then resolved series of actions and events. For a clearer picture of how a film may continue narrating such general story material *after* the major action has been resolved, we might imagine a version of *The Quiet Man* that did not end after Sean and Mary Kate wave at the camera. If that film continued after Sean and Mary Kate's happiness was assured with the inclusion of a series of shots and sounds unrelated to the story of Sean and Mary Kate, (such as shots of the sky, anonymous buildings, and unidentified people milling about at a soccer game), the film would be an Open Discourse text. The clouds and people would be the "told" level of the narration, yet their inclusion, like an abstract series of images, would neither continue the story of Sean and Mary Kate nor constitute a second story. But the unlikelihood of finding such a fiction film now becomes clear since adding "material" that neither relates to the previous story nor begins another one, would hardly seem to count as narrative. How can Story be resolved when Discourse continues presenting more material?

An additional challenge for the Open Discourse category brought up by this hypothetical *Quiet Man* expansion is the role of the audience in interpreting the end of these films. It is difficult to imagine a final segment of a film that could not be read as some sort of metaphorical epilogue underlining an established theme. As the Kuleshov experiments reportedly proved in their test of viewer extrapolation of meaning out of the sequential presentation of disparate images, the spectator's desire to connect images and sounds into cause-effect relationships is a central part of film viewing. The conventions and norms of all but the most experimental of films would seem to indicate to the audience that films are unified on some level. Moreover, the termination effect of trying to read the end of a film back into the text as a whole would suggest that it would be difficult to posit a final series of shots that could not be interpreted in some way as continuing or at least commenting thematically upon the preceding story.

Descriptive Open Discourse Films

In general, it appears that there are two ways that a narrative discourse could continue narrating without continuing the same story or opening up a second, completely new story. The first method would involve *descriptive* narration, while the second would be *abstract* narration. A descriptive epilogue would be one that could not propel the narrative further but instead simply displayed objects or locations (autonomous story elements), that may or may not have been shown earlier in the film. The abstract ending would be one that continued some purely formal play of the narration, abandoning the representational conventions established throughout the rest of the film. In this chapter on the Open Discourse film it will be necessary to define the story's resolution and the production by the narrative discourse. In Paul Ricoeur's analysis of ambiguous or "difficult" literary endings, he raises a point that must be kept in mind during the isolation of the primary story from the final activity of the narrative discourse. Ricoeur notes that endings are often difficult to classify: "One difficulty comes from the ever-present confusion between the end of the imitated action and the end of the fiction as such."[4] Separating descriptive or abstract elements from those which might support, underline, comment upon, or actively continue earlier story events is a constant threat to this critical activity.

But it is time to become more concrete and deal with specific films to illustrate various strategies for using a descriptive syntagma (or even a system of descriptive syntagmas) to end an Open Discourse film. Our first example is Hal Ashby's *Being There* (1979), while the second is Claude Chabrol's *Les Bonnes femmes* (1960). *Being There* is a curious example of a film with an end title sequence that has a completely independent narrative function from the rest of the film. While the film's fictional level concerns the trials and tribulations of the simple-minded Chance Gardener, the end title sequence is a collection of "blooper" out-takes from the film, showing Peter Sellers, as Chance, missing cues, giggling, and bungling his lines.

The addition of this final section, which shows comical versions of a scene already witnessed in the film, serves as a revelation of the

115

filmmaking process, that also, ironically, undercuts the serious satire. But the sequence's second function involves providing an homage to Peter Sellers who died during *Being There*'s post-production. Thus the entire ending has no bearing on the already accomplished resolution of the fiction: Chance Gardener is about to be nominated for President at the end of the story. Yet the out-takes allow the film to continue narrating story elements that act as a final salute to the real, nondiegetic Peter Sellers.

This example is "descriptive" in that it continues the narrative discourse by presenting a series of scene fragments in a rhetorical order meant to reveal the personality of Sellers, while also making a statement on the nature of film production itself. The end sequence shows the audience the labor of the late Sellers just as descriptively as *Citizen Kane*'s opening newsreel sequence presented the life of the fictional Kane. But the end of *Being There* is unique in that it was tacked onto an otherwise Closed Text film to dedicate retrospectively the film to Peter Sellers. *Being There* provides a model of how a shift in narrating strategies could add a very different end sequence onto a narrative film without continuing the already resolved story, yet it is more of a documentary tribute than fictional strategy here. Nonetheless, this ending is more radically open than the tacked on sections concluding films like *Butch Cassidy and the Sundance Kid* (Hill, 1969) or *Thelma and Louise* (Scott, 1991). Both these films add montages of earlier story events in order as ways to both summarize the lives of their characters and to undercut the bitterness of their sudden, freeze-frame deaths. Thus the latter two examples provide descriptive story material that *does* reinforce narrative closure and thus they belong solidly to Closed Text traditions.

Chabrol's *Les Bonnes femmes* provides a very different attempt to continue the narration once the actual story is resolved. In *Les Bonnes femmes*, four women who work together in an electrical goods shop pursue their individual paths toward happiness: Rita (Lucille Saint-Simon) is engaged to a dull but solid bourgeois man, Ginette (Stephane Audran) sings secretly, Jane (Bernadette Lafont) lives wildly, pursuing chance encounters, and Jacqueline (Clotilde Joano) waits patiently for pure love to arrive in the form of a modern Prince Charming. *Les bonnes femmes* ends rather dramatically yet arbitrarily: the dreamy, naive Jacqueline is strangled by her boyfriend André (Mario David) in the woods, his motorcycle is seen by a troop of boy scouts, and André drops a scarf as he rides away. Thus the film establishes the probability of André's eventual capture (there are eyewitnesses and a material clue), yet all of that is left unresolved. We never even see Jacqueline's three friends learn of her death. However, while the story stops with André's flight from the scene of the crime, the film does not yet end there; instead there is a brief final sequence of a young woman dancing somewhere that cannot be tied to the immediate diegetic world of Chabrol's story about four women. James Monaco describes the end this way: "That *Les Bonnes femmes* is meant as a generalization is re-emphasized by its closing sequence: in a dance hall a young woman is picked up. She smiles and dances with the man. We never see his face, only hers—and the slowly revolving mirrored ball that hangs from the ceiling."[5]

This ending gives the viewer no reason to suspect that André is indeed the unseen man, since André's seduction of Jacqueline was slow and methodical and he has always been identified with the out of doors rather than the glittery world of night clubs. Instead, the ending becomes more metaphoric, relating to the *theme* of *Les Bonnes femmes*, but not specifically resolving the action of any of the four women portrayed in the film. Gavin Millar, for instance, describes the end as even more ironic: "A final image leaves us with a fifth girl, a stranger, eternally hopeful, dancing under a sphere of revolving mirrors in a ballroom."[6] Millar's description, like Monaco's, cites the revolving mirrored ball as a key informant, and the ball may thus be interpreted as a metaphor for the film as a whole (providing brief glimpses of the details of several women's lives) as well as recalling the opening sequence in which Jane (Bernadette Lafont) was picked up by two married men at a nightclub. The end then brackets partially the film by recalling the opening seduction of Jane, but cannot be so easily interpreted as hopeful; the film's moody pessimism is actually further underlined with the anonymous victim about to repeat the cycle of Jane, Ginette, and Jacqueline.

Robin Wood's account of *Les Bonnes femmes* breaks the film into only seven segments, the last of which is this sequence of the unnamed girl in the nightclub. Wood acknowledges that the final scene "stands apart from all that has gone before in terms of narrative structure: the characters are entirely new, and the time-continuity is abruptly broken for the first time in the film."[7] This final sequence ends the formal play of light and dark in the figure of the revolving mirror ball, according to Wood, and while the fifth girl does not affect the lives of the other four, "she too, perhaps, is trapped in a dream she will never be able to fulfil."[8] There is, as a result, a *thematic* parallel between the last woman and the preceding four, but on the level of actual story action the final scene has no bearing on their story. Wood concludes that the final scene makes the film formally "much more complex and 'open'"[9] than other Chabrol other films.

One of the most perceptive of Chabrol's critics is Joel Magny who finds the final scene goes beyond simple thematics to unveil cinematic and social parameters at work. For Magny, the film's replacement of the other women with an anonymous young woman in a social setting suddenly shifts Chabrol's project. Centering finally on the spinning ball, a shimmering device breaking light into hundreds of beams, reveals "the illusion that nourished the characters but also that which feeds the cinema and spectator. Crime here renders the social order as guilty but is also at the heart of the contract we each sign by buying movie tickets."[10] The final sequence abandons the specific thematics of *Les Bonnes femmes* and creates a pessimistic epilogue concerning crime, voyeurism, and cinematic spectacle.

The example of *Les Bonnes femmes* as an Open Discourse film is imperfect in that the addition of the fifth, unidentified woman does serve the film's theme of the pathos and fragility in the women's naive, desperate hopes. Moreover, the earlier story, much like an Open Story film, leaves some plot points unresolved. Nonetheless, the film does suggest a variation of the Open Discourse film in that *Les Bonnes femmes*, unlike *The 400 Blows*, is provisionally resolved with Jacqueline's murder, which Monaco summarizes as "André's quiet—almost sacrificial—execution" which has "an air of inevitability."[11] But then a final segment presents new story elements that can only be related metaphorically to the stories of Ginette, Rita, Jane, Jacqueline, or André. The degree of resolution here is low, yet the addition of the discontinuous last segment (the preceding story time involves roughly 36 consecutive hours) allows the rest of the film to look complete in contrast to this final discursively open section. Here then, Chabrol's film foregrounds the spectator's role in perceiving closure: it would be difficult for a viewer not to interpret the fifth woman as thematically linked to the other four "bonnes femmes" yet this fifth, anonymous woman in some anonymous place simultaneously seems completely excessive to their tale.

One issue thus crucial to outlining the descriptive Open Discourse films is the role played by the spectator in assigning thematic resolution to a film. Victor Shklovsky is one critic whose observations on reader expectations help us understand the role interpretation plays in the constant struggle to integrate these excessive endings into their already resolved stories. He argues that the use of epilogues helps conclude the narrative, and that even purely descriptive epilogues can often be incorporated into the theme and textual structure by the readers, creating a sort of "illusory ending." As an example, Shklovsky includes mention of the descriptions of nature and even the weather, as they "furnish material for these illusory endings."[12] According to Shklovsky, even rather neutral literary motifs at the close of a novel or short story may be interpreted by the spectator as an anchoring element to complete the theme, or make a final, significant comment on the preceding story action and resolution. Thus, the final images of the fifth woman in *Les Bonnes femmes* might be tied tightly to the preceding story by the spectator *even though* they do not include any recognized characters or locations. As a result, an excessive independent sequence may be used by the spectator as a key to re-reading the preceding story, or as a terminating narrative comment or epilogue. A viewer's struggle to integrate such an ending actually creates a textual tension, undercutting such a sequence's radical potential to disrupt closure.

An example of a film that fits closer to Shklovsky's weather and nature descriptions may be Dovzhenko's *Earth* (1929). Like *Les Bonnes femmes*, *Earth* is not a pure example of an Open Discourse film, but only suggests how a film might be interpreted as satisfying some of the requirements of a narrative that continues after its major story events are resolved. The final sequence of Dovzhenko's *Earth* creates a symbolic, non-diegetic scene of apples, watermelons, and other fruits in their natural settings during a rain shower. This sequence does repeat and expand a similar segment of shots from earlier in the film, yet the montage does not resolve any strict story events, it simply reflects upon them. At the end of *Earth*, the young Communist, Vasyl, has just been buried, then there is a series of fruit shots, and finally, Vasyl's girlfriend is shown hugging some anonymous young man in an unnamed time and place.

In order to prove that the end of *Earth*, like that of *Les Bonnes femmes*, approaches Open Discourse status, we need to look more closely at that film's cyclical structure. *Earth* can be divided into ten sequences, the first of which begins with a series of shots that will be repeated at the film's close: there are four shots of the hill of wheat, a shot of a young woman standing in a sunflower field (see fig. 4.1), a close-up of a sunflower itself, then six shots of apples in a tree, and a shot of an elderly man. While the sunflowers will not be repeated often within the film, the hill will be the stage for future action since it is literally the field of battle between the landowners and peasants; the field is also the place from which Foma Belokon[13] (grandson of the old gentleman) will declare his guilt in killing Vasyl.

Similarly, the opening scene's apple shots set up the fruit as the literal "fruit of the land," becoming a symbol for fertility, productivity, and livelihood. The final request of Semyon, the dying man, is to eat an apple. Next, Semyon lies down to die among harvested apples, and the children eat apples as he slowly succumbs. Piotr, a comical old farmer who believes Semyon will speak to him from his grave, is on hand for Semyon's demise, and represents the silly superstitions of the "powerful" landowners.

During the second scene, Foma is shown to be an enemy of the people for hoarding land and supplies (he threatens to kill his horse to prevent the Collective from taking it). Next, during the third scene, Vasyl and his hardworking father argue over the future, with Vasyl proclaiming that his Communist cell will bring a tractor for the Collective and thereby literally take the earth away from the rich farmers. This scene ends with the father, impressed with the Communists' spunk and ideas, eating fruit. Nonetheless, scene 4 portrays Vasyl's father Opanas as a cynical farmer. Opanas trusts only in his own labor and his oxen, while his optimistic son goes off in search of a tractor. In addition, old Piotr is mocked by the children during this scene for asking the dead Semyon's grave what it is like "over there."

Scenes 5 and 6 show Vasyl arriving with the tractor (see fig. 4.2), Foma threatening Vasyl, and finally Vasyl plowing up the land after having promised the Collective that they will indeed prosper. Scene 6 includes the montage of Vasyl plowing, the women joyously collecting the wheat, and then a sort of rain of wheat being harvested. Finally this harvest montage ends with cross-cutting between the earth being churned by the tractor's plow, bread dough kneaded by machinery, and hundreds of loaves of bread being baked. Prosperity has arrived thanks to Vasyl, the Communist cell, and the tractor.

In scene 7, there is a night at first full of happiness and sexual promise among the young people (a soft-focus shot of a man with his hand on a woman's breast, standing in the fields under a harvest moon), but then the heroic Vasyl is killed by Foma while dancing for joy on a road late that night. In scene 8, the people, and especially Vasyl's girlfriend, mourn this death with the newly politicized Opanas accusing the landowners of killing his son. Opanas finally decides that since Vasyl died for a "new world" he should be buried in a new way, without the Church. In scene 9 the struggle is thus saved by old Opanas, the

Fig. 4.1. *Earth*. Vasyl's girlfriend and sunflower

Fig. 4.2. Vasyl on the tractor

formerly skeptical peasant, as he finds a new faith in the collectivization of the land and allows the cell leader to replace the priest at the funeral. The funeral procession becomes an outpouring of peasants and Vasyl's open casket is carried past orchards and sunflower fields. During the funeral, Foma, dancing hysterically and spinning on the hill and among the gravestones, declares his guilt, but the people ignore him, watching instead a Communist airplane in the sky overhead (see fig. 4.3).

At this point, there is a shot of the hill of wheat, but Foma is suddenly absent, as if he has literally vanished from the land. Next, there is a montage of 31 shots of apples, watermelons, and other fruits in the fields, during a rainstorm (see fig. 4.4). Following these shots there is a graphic match from a round fruit to a shot of the girlfriend's head, then a shot of a young man, gazing down, then there is a shot of the woman awakening and seeing him, and in the final image of the film this new couple hugs in a concluding two-shot.

Dovzhenko's films, and *Earth* in particular, are regularly discussed in terms of their lyricism, and their combination of the real and mythical. The end of *Earth* resembles that of the undying soldier finale of *Arsenal*: here the spirit of Vasyl survives in the form of an anonymous young man. According to Jean and Luda Schnitzer, the end of *Earth* is quite straightforward, acting as a celebration of Vasyl's efforts: "Vasyl smiles in his coffin while the branches of the apples trees caress his face. A welcome storm cries for the death and laughs at life. Vasyl has triumphed and death can do nothing about it. . . . He is immortal since he has given his life that the future may live."[14]

Thus, the Schnitzers call attention to Dovzhenko's stylistic combination of the real, the imaginary, and the purely fantastic, yet their account of the ending of *Earth* narrativizes the storm too strongly. It is certainly true that the storm is portrayed as responding to Vasyl's death, but it is not anchored to the time or space of Vasyl's funeral. Moreover, there is no indication that the Collective needs rain, thus even the degree to which the rain is "welcome" is not certain. The storm is welcomed by the spectator since it indeed offers a gentle, fertile, and visually pleasing series of images, yet it is less the storm that renders Vasyl immortal, than the speech by the cell leader who declares that Vasyl's glory will circle the earth like the Communist airplane flying overhead.

The Schnitzers' account of *Earth* also makes a metaphoric leap in declaring that the apple branches caress Vasyl's smiling face. This direct link of the apple trees to Vasyl again ties the rain and fruit montage too

Fig. 4.3. Foma dances madly in the cemetery

Fig. 4.4. Watermelons in final fruit montage

tightly to the concrete narrative action. Vasyl, dead in his coffin, is not seen during the bulk of the funeral scene, instead, the images feature the cell leader, Opanas, the crowd, and Foma Belokon. Vasyl's dead but smiling face is never shown near the end of the funeral sequence, nor at the beginning of the fruit montage. Therefore, it is only on a very metaphorical level that the fruit and rain sequence can be said to cry over or "caress" the dead Vasyl. The association of Vasyl with the rain montage is primarily due to the order of the sequences, with the rain and fruit following the funeral scene.

The point behind this discussion of the Schnitzers' account of *Earth* is certainly not to quibble over readings of the end of the film. Instead, it offers the rain montage as an example of an eccentric narrative tactic which forces spectators to connect it to Vasyl's life and death. While a summary like that of the Schnitzers' tends to reduce the folkloric epilogue merely to serving the resolution of the story, it may be more accurate to consider the montage as a narrational strategy that repeats and builds upon earlier motifs from the film's narrative discourse. There is a decisive difference between an apple branch caressing the cheek of the protagonist, and a montage of apples that comes after the protagonist's funeral. In both cases the montage must be linked to the whole metaphoric theme of the film, yet the story line is resolved at the end of the funeral scene while the formal, narrational play of the primary narrator continues in the form of the montage.

The return of the apple sequence at the close of *Earth*, continues working out the more metaphoric level of the film's narration, going beyond the time, space, and events of the film's story proper. Dovzhenko's lyrical story telling, which Leyda calls "so slight as to be almost plotless,"[15] nonetheless establishes patterns that are not bound closely to the story. Yet these patterns exist on a discursive plane separate from the immediate character, actions, or places of the story. On a very general thematic level, the film can be said to be about death, hence Ivor Montagu's remark, cited by Leyda, that death is the key to the film, is quite accurate: "Death apprehended never as an end, a finish, dust to dust. But death as a sacrifice . . . a part of the unending process of reviving life."[16] The apples and rain use both textual links (Semyon's death surrounded by apples) and extratextual connotations (soft, steady rain symbolizing sadness, loss, and the life cycle) to close off the thematic development of the film.

It is possible, therefore, to read the apple montage as a discursive sequence that comes after the story's primary resolution (Vasyl's funeral unites the Communists, Opanas, and the peasants as they all literally watch their bright future flying overhead like Vasyl's soul transformed into an airplane). The montage becomes excessive for the story's resolution, but formally possible since it concludes a pattern developed throughout the film, and it helps bracket the film by loosely mirroring the beginning.

If the final four images of Vasyl's girlfriend were not included, *Earth* would be a clearer example of the Open Discourse film.[17] Moving from a resolved story at the point of Vasyl's funeral, to the fruit sequence would act as both a descriptive and thematic Open Discourse ending, but adding shots of the two lovers united after Vasyl's death returns us to the story and does give a sort of story epilogue: The story is re-resolved as Vasyl's girlfriend overcomes her loss and the people prosper, and the narrative discourse closes off the narrative. Thus, rather than being a film with an inconclusive narrative discourse, *Earth* moves toward being an Open Discourse film in that its narrative discourse continues after the story is resolved, but its discourse does not remain "open." Without the final, mythical termination, the fruit montage would indeed serve as a discursive and thematic segment that continued beyond the resolution of the primary story line involving Vasyl, the Belokon family and the future of the Collective, and *Earth* would be a better example of an Open Discourse.

In a prototype Open Discourse film like *Les Bonnes femmes* and *Earth*, what follows the story resolution is not completely predictable, and therefore the power of these films derives from challenging the conventions of efficient closure by reasserting the productivity and unique style of the text's narrative discourse. The spectator, however, will probably make an effort in each of these films to relate the final scenes on a metaphoric level to the story that has come before. Godard's *Tout va bien* (1972) supplies a further example of a film on its way to becoming more open in its final moments even though the spectator may very well relate the last section of that film to many motifs raised earlier.

The story of *Tout va bien* revolves around the personal careers and politics of Jacques (Yves Montand) and Susan (Jane Fonda). This primary and most strongly unifying narrative strand is finally resolved in a pair of parodic cafe scenes. The real degree of resolution in *Tout va bien* is left somewhat suspended, or at least threatened, when the film returns to a voice-over discussion between a man and woman who speak about the task of ending this film. These voices began the film by explaining the prerequisites and constraints involved in making a movie (money, a story, stars), and now the voices return to "lay bare the device," by calling attention to the artifice and economics of film production. During this next-to-last scene of the film, Susan and Jacques are reunited on one level, even while their status as characters is simultaneously undercut by the voice-over discussion.

In her analysis of the Brechtian strategies at work within *Tout va bien*, Kristin Thompson analyzes the film's ending:

> Again, the film is not a natural thing, but a construct, and as such can end in different ways. Godard and Gorin present two alternative endings—Jacques waits for Susan, She waits for Him—but even then they make it clear that these particular choices are dictated by the social need for a happy ending to the love story. But *Tout va bien* has not been simply a Hollywood romance; the couple gets back together, but the woman's voice states: 'We'll simply say that He and She have begun to rethink themselves in historical terms.'[18]

Thompson's citation of the film's ending is helpful in setting up the double resolution of this film's story: either Jacques waits in the cafe and Susan arrives, or the opposite occurs. Yet while the resolution is repeated with the characters having switched places, it still operates as two instances of the same final story action, which is the reuniting, or starting over, of the couple. The voice-over commentary reinforces this resolution by acting as a framing closure device. Just as voice-overs began the film, speaking of the constraints and components of filmmaking, they now return to wrap up the drama. The woman says, "And the spectator will say they went through a crisis," while the male voice adds, "Let us each be our own historian."

Tout va bien does not end, however, with the voice-over conversation about Jacques and Susan. Instead, the song "France—1972," starts up and there is chanting on the soundtrack, soon joined by the male voice-over stating, "me, you." The image cuts away from Jacques and Susan to a tracking shot through an industrial Paris suburb. Among the crowd's chants are parts of a communist labor union speech that blend with other crowd noises to give a very full soundtrack which suggests a large population on the move. The male voice finally says, "We'll live more carefully—me, you, her, us." The end titles, "Ter/min/ée," and the intertitle announcing that this has been a tale for those who do not have one, finally put the film to rest.

This final section of *Tout va bien*, during the last tracking shot, acts as an extra scene that does not further the drama of Jacques and Susan's relationship. While this final scene could be read as an extension of that couple's working out of difficulties (so that just as they are working together by confronting their problems, the working class and leftist intellectuals are doing the same), the tracking shot and sounds are not directly connected to Jacques and Susan any more than the rain and fruit were tied to the dead Vasyl. *Tout va bien* could have ended with the voices over the relatively conclusive cafe scene, but instead this filmic appendix continues the narrative discourse.

One way to interpret *Tout va bien* is that personal politics are inseparable from a larger sphere, thus the final track opens up the story's realm, while it also becomes a visual pun on taking theory into the streets. The end, therefore, goes beyond the simple description of details or places in the environment, and instead becomes a political essay-like maneuver. Nonetheless, the final shot and its accompanying soundtrack do force the narrative discourse to reopen after the cafe scene, breaking the final bracket that had been set up to mirror the film's opening.

The ending of *Tout va bien* suggests another variation of the descriptive Open Discourse film conclusion. *Tout va bien* only begins what should, for our purposes at least, be a longer, more autonomous film segment in order to supply a really clear, independent final narrational section. The ending of *Tout va bien*, however, does move parallel to the preceding story's themes, so may be integrated partially by the spectator into that story. Nevertheless, the final tracking shot does move independently of any character, and provides a stronger example of how narration can operate without continuing the preceding story. If the final section of *Tout va bien* does act as a variation on an essayist's epilogue, this epilogue exists only on an abstract, intellectual level beyond that of the story concerning Jacques and Susan. The end reaches beyond their story because the space of this street has never been linked to either Jacques or Susan, and there is no cue that the tracking shot is their point of view. Instead, the final shot sequence may be more like what the original Godard-voice had in mind from the beginning: a film without characters, without a story, and without a studio.

In order for an Open Discourse film to work it does not need a final section that is completely isolated from the preceding text. The Open Discourse ending does, however, need to supply the viewer with a conclusion that continues narrative systems but not story events. In *Tout va bien*, the spectator may relate the "France—1972" song, and the chants that accompany it, to the overall themes of class struggle. Jean-

Pierre Gorin, the film's co-director, interprets the final tracking shot and soundtrack as conclusive of several formal and thematic threads that unify the film: "Of course the last tracking shot sums up the whole film—the slum landscape with that incredible song. You pass along the wall, and on the soundtrack you have the three principal sounds of the film—the leftist sound, the Communist Party sound, the boss sound. They're like sound vignettes stamped on that bare wall. . . . That's the summary of the film."[19] While it may not be as easy as Gorin suggests to perceive the three different sounds, much less relate them to specific political voices, the narrative discourse nevertheless continues the film's ideas without any longer using the story elements as supports.

Indeed there is also another way to read this final image that goes beyond simply interpreting the suburbs as the present or future battleground for class struggle: Instead of seeing the final scene as a call to action, or a summation, there is the fact that the empty image is also an ironic negation of the soundtrack. We may hear representatives of the working class, yet we see no one actually listening nor even moving in those neighborhoods. Perhaps the call to action is either misdirected or has proven ineffective.

From the examples of *Les Bonnes femmes*, *Earth*, and *Tout va bien*, the Open Discourse film begins to become a more useful concept. The key element of their narration is that their stories' resolutions are followed by sounds and images not directly related to those preceding resolutions. The events seen and heard do, in fact, continue the narration, yet they do not open a new trajectory for the stories. The spectator is exposed to sounds and images no longer strictly connected to a new story, nor to the old resolved story's action, and the film finally ends when there are no more of these sounds or images being projected.

The Abstract Open Discourse Film

The second Open Discourse type, the Abstract film, employs a final section that may accomplish some of the same functions of the Descriptive film (such as sustaining or challenging the mood or theme), but with less representational signifiers. Like the Descriptive Open Discourse films, the abstract films may incorporate sounds and/or images from earlier in the film, as long as those textual elements do not establish an additional story tacked onto the first. Before considering all the problems inherent with defining this sub-category, however, it will be helpful to consider an example of a film that prefigures some of the strategies of an abstract Open Discourse film.

Bresson's *Pickpocket* (1959) stands as a limited example of a film whose ending begins to approach the Open Discourse text's lack of narrative closure. Throughout *Pickpocket*, voice-over narration and sequential action keep the film relatively unified and linear. At the film's end, Michel and Jeanne realize that their lives are, in fact, tied together, and they exchange reverential kisses through the prison visitors' screen. At this point the story is resolved and the music begins to swell. Next Michel's narration concludes by mentioning how long it has taken him to come to Jeanne and there is a slow fade to black. The "end" title fades in and out, yet the music continues for one full minute over black leader.

By resolving the story, but continuing the musical theme (even after "the end" titles), Bresson's film achieves a doubling effect that is similar to a conventional epilogue, since it re-enforces the story's end. The music is severe, celebrating their mutual affection, yet it also underlines the tragedy of the story which is brought on by Michel's very late realization that he has erred. The music acts like the theme music under conventional end credits, in that it works to solidify the conclusiveness of the narrative discourse's textual construction. What is different about *Pickpocket*, however, is that the music is not accompanied by any end titles, but simply continues alone. This use of music is in keeping with Bresson's observation that the sound and image tracks must not repeat one another.[20] In effect, *Pickpocket*'s closing music serves the same function that additional shots of the devoted couple Jeanne and Michel could also accomplish: it augments the other closure devices and completes the story's final action by rendering it permanent and eternal.

The end music for *Pickpocket*, therefore, is not an unmotivated or excessive narrative device. If the end music came *before* the end title, however, placing itself as a final formal element, it would move the film's termination closer to the Open Discourse text. By following the final image with one or two minutes of black leader accompanied only by music, the narrative discourse is indeed exceeding story. One could certainly imagine story resolution which was completed during the end music only. If, for instance, Michel was to be executed soon after seeing Jeanne, and the music was punctuated by the sound of the guillotine falling, the soundtrack would produce what the image track could not, or would not, reveal: the main character's death. The closing music in *Pickpocket*, however, simply echoes the final images, but without adding new story events or actions. The soundtrack in Bresson's film continues after the story's resolution, though it admittedly accentuates that very resolution as an unusual, but functional, closure device.

The interest in *Pickpocket*, like the discussion of *Tout va bien*, centers on the fact that it offers one possible glimpse at the shape and narrative function of Open Discourse strategies. Jonas Mekas's *Notes on the Circus*, when viewed independently of *Diaries, Notes and Sketches*, has a similar ending to that of *Pickpocket*, because the final circus music continues after the last images of the circus. In both cases the music and black leader call attention to the arbitrariness of closure and the power of the narrator in the process of narrative conclusion.

Following a story's resolution with an unusually long period of black leader and a stretch of nondiegetic music may appear to be a weak example of abstraction. In Bresson's cinema, however, theme music acts as moderately autonomous narration. Moreover, the music at the close of the film serves a stylistic rather than strictly narrative function. Still, the true Open Discourse text would have to go further, foregrounding some formal play, via music, the rhythmic cutting together of non-representational images, and/or the combination of identifiable sounds or images into sequences following principles other than those of narrative logic or description. An Open Discourse film that moves from a resolved story to abstract textual production contradicts principles of both narrative unity and motivation. Hence it becomes a radically signifying text. In fact, this inclusion of a final sequence that threatens or changes the norms of narration established in the previous narrative portion of the film, would challenge the larger generic divisions between fiction, documentary, and experimental cinema.

By now it should come as no great surprise, therefore, to discover that there may be no strict examples of narrative films that complete a resolved story, yet then continue with images or sounds that cannot be interpreted as motivated by that narrative. Obviously such a film could be both confusing and troubling. As mentioned earlier, Bordwell writes that viewers make sense of classical films by considering verisimilitude (is x plausible?), generic appropriateness (is x characteristic of this sort of film?) and compositional unity (does x advance the story?).[21] The abstract Open Discourse film would have the spectator answering "no" on all three counts, and an unrealistic, inappropriate, and disunifying strategy would necessarily be the basic characteristic of these films. The abstract ending would refer the spectator to an entirely different set of norms or backgrounds. The most extreme art cinema norms of ambiguity or authorial intervention would perhaps be the only justification for such sequences ("Oh you know Chabrol, he likes to add a flicker film at the end of his narratives.")

In the abstract Open Discourse film, the linearity of the story progression would no longer be the driving force behind the text, as the productivity, style, and specificity of the narrative discourse would dominate the film's ending. In his discussion of generic plot resolution, Thomas Schatz points out four large textual activities: the establishment of conflicts, animation of conflicts, intensification of the drama, and resolution.[22] The very order of these four narrative components reinforces closure. Adding "abstraction" after resolution would quickly derail the direct path toward narrative termination. Theorizing the active presence of abstract images and nondiegetic sounds after a story is resolved helps us understand better stable vs. unstable closure, and offers a glimpse at how narrative film would have to fuse with experimental film in order to satisfy the conditions of a truly abstract Open Discourse film ending.

Conclusions

Finally, one aspect of the Open Discourse film that must be considered is the problem of what these narrative strategies would accomplish beyond simply contradicting conventions of storytelling. According to Ricoeur, one characteristic of modernism is precisely this undercutting of the stability of ending a narrative: "It is legitimate to take the abandonment of the criterium of completion, and thus the purposeful decision to leave a work unfinished, as symptoms of the end of the tradition of *mise en intrigue*."[23] While Open Text films like *Weekend* choose one strategy to emphasize the potential for narrative to challenge both the notions of a resolved story and a closed narration, the Open Discourse film works slightly differently; these films have to deliver a resolved story while at the same time going beyond it.

The most fascinating theoretical aspect of Open Discourse films, beyond trying to find in practice a text that fits the theoretical definition, is the spectator's role in struggling to connect excessive discursive tactics with story tactics, thereby unifying a text which is itself fighting toward disunity. The hypothesis-making and retrospective reading would seem to allow the spectator to try relating every narrative element and stylistic strategy to the story. After all, we are quite prepared to apply problem-solving processes to challenging art films. Thus it would be quite unusual for the audience to grant simply that the final section of a narrative film as excessive and autonomous without managing to justify it on some grounds.

In spite of the resolution of a story's major action code, the spectator's past experience will have cued him/her to interpret every aspect, no matter how descriptive or abstract, to the narrative. Even the "tone," therefore, of an Open Discourse film's final section could be retrospectively hooked back thematically or metaphorically into the film's story. For instance, such endings could be interpreted as paralleling "lost" or directionless characters. Or, more rarely, Open Discourse endings could be interpreted formally as allowing the audience a bit of structured "free" time to let the ending "sink in," as may be the case for some viewers at *Pickpocket*. Thus the Open Discourse film may be rare or even impossible in cinematic spectating practice precisely because the audience's viewing norms are so far removed from accepting a section of a narrative film as unrelated to all that came before it.

One film example that helps us see the difficulty is isolating an Open Discourse film and helps us shift from this category to the Open text is Ingmar Bergman's *Persona* (1966). *Persona* begins with a famous dream-like series of images that has been interpreted as excessive to the film and as its key and as a subjective vision whose source can never be isolated. Among other things, the opening includes parts of a film projector, leader, primitive animation, a sheep being sacrificed, a hand hammered with a nail, old bodies in a morgue, and a young boy in a similar white room reaching out to a screen projecting a woman's face. Once this prologue is finished, the titles roll and the story of actress Elizabet Vogler (Liv Ullman) and her nurse Alma (Bibi Andersson) begins.

What makes *Persona* so interesting an example for this study is that some of Bergman's oneiric images return in a final brief montage at the end. There are shots of Bergman and Sven Nykvist filming what is apparently Elisabet / Liv Ullman, the boy reaching out to the woman's face, and a projector breaking down, and the carbon arcs going black to darken the screen. If this film had told a resolved tale of Anna and Elisabet and then tacked on these images we would have a clearly Open Discourse film. However, there story is never really resolved. Questions abound concerning what, if anything, was settled in this very open story: Was the husband there? Did Alma lose her sanity and was Elisabet at all cured? Which parts were subjective visions, and whose? Moreover, Bergman further fragments their story with intrusive nondiegetic images. As Marilyn Johns Blackwell writes, "The fiction fades and only artifice remains. . . . The film emerges out of and descends back into nothingness."[24] *Persona*, with its dreamy blurring of the lines between subject, fiction, and narration reveals how unlikely it would be to have a conventionally resolved story followed by an excessive discursive epilogue.

As we will see in the next chapter, the Open Text's discontinuous stories allow the narration to play with the conventions of narrativity throughout a film, while this chapter has shown that the Open Discourse films, by contrast, tell a much more resolved story. But an abstract or descriptive coda at the end of an Open Discourse film achieves some of the same modernist goals as the Open Text films, thus the end result is to reveal that story is only one function of narrative. Narrative discourse need not simply shape and resolve the story, but may continue narrating after the story's resolution.

The stories in *Les Bonnes femmes*, *Tout va bien*, *Earth*, and *Pickpocket*, are certainly the central aspects of those films. Yet the open systems at the ends of those films call attention to the discursive choices made by their narrative strategies as they once again foreground the filmic *écriture* as equal in significance and productivity to the story being told. As we will see in the next chapter, discussion of the Open Discourse film has been important in establishing processes and characteristics that will help analyze the role filmic strategies of openness play in Open Text narration.

CHAPTER 5

THE OPEN TEXT FILM

It is impossible for any author to reassure the spectator who is
apprehensive about the fate of the hero after the words 'the
end.' After the word 'end,' by definition, nothing else
happens. The only future that the work could accept is
another identical screening; place the film reels back on the
film projector.

—Alain Robbe-Grillet[1]

The analyses so far have revealed three kinds of endings—the Closed
Text, Open Story, and Open Discourse films. We now need to examine
the fourth category of Open Text films. Throughout this study the
fourth type of ending stands as a sort of end point in itself, as the most
extreme narrative strategy, because these films are marked by both an
unresolved story and an incomplete closure of their narrative discourse.
Even the Open Text films, however, have not achieved a truly open film
structure or ending. This goal, like Barthes's concept of the *scriptible*
text,[2] is perhaps impossible to attain. In spite of Frank Kermode's claim
that no narrative can truly avoid being a "completed action,"[3] we must
account for films that do strive to be writerly, unconventionally organized, and inconclusive, with gaps and inconsistencies in both their story
and its telling. In the end, the Open Text film is always partly about what
a narrative is, and thus about how films end and how viewers create
meaning.

In a physical sense every narrative film does end, yet Godard's
Weekend (1967) certainly lacks *The Quiet Man*'s completeness and unity.
By looking at how story irresolution and discursive openness function
it will be easier to understand how the more open films by Godard,
Chantal Akerman, or Alain Robbe-Grillet differ in their narration from

films of the preceding categories. To a certain degree, these films spring from sources as diverse as surrealism, formalism, experimental cinema, and the *nouveau roman* school of the 1950s: they try to sidestep the traditional story, plotting, and temporal/spatial logic of more conventional narratives, thereby becoming what Peter Brooks would label "fictions of fiction making."[4] Because of these strategies, Open Text films often fragment character development and even break down the very operation of story, plot, and action while challenging conventions of omniscient, objective, or monological narration.

These films work to construct new narrative structures that demand new kinds of endings. Unlike Open Story films, Open Text films go beyond simple ambiguity or narrative *mise-en-abimes*. It is no longer only the story's end that remains ambiguous or suspended, instead the narration itself is called into question both during and at the end of the film. One of the motivating forces behind filmmakers like Godard, Akerman, or Chris Marker was the desire to stop working within the ideological constraints of the commercial narrative cinema. Similarly, the events of May 1968 in France and Western Europe as a whole brought together many diverse political and artistic influences, from Bertolt Brecht to Louis Althusser, that would turn attention toward a widespread questioning of conventional film language, as well as commercial production and distribution channels. As Jean-Luc Comolli and Jean Narboni write, filmmakers began to recognize the ideological implications of conventional film style and techniques: "Only action on both fronts, 'signified' and 'signifiers,' has any hope of operating against the prevailing ideology."[5]

Thus Godard's own statement that people need to make "political films politically" relates to this larger artistic movement of devising new rules for textual production, thereby circumventing conventional relations between author, text, and spectator. The production of Open Text films, therefore, satisfies many modernist trends by offering films that cannot fit easily into the mold of a completed art product. As Armine Kotin Mortimer argues, "Modern texts have invented new forms to avoid or bypass the necessity of closure. . . . [Such] texts do not want to end."[6] Open Text films spring from aesthetic and political traditions that evade dominant ideological forms of the narrative film, just as the Closed Text films could be argued to reinforce dominant aesthetic and ideological modes of representation. Once a text challenges finality on story and discursive levels, narrative time, space, logic, and voice all become shifting forces rather than conclusive forms. After all, if we accept Hayden White's claim that narrative is informed by the moral authority of the narrator, then when that narrator questions its own power and status, social and textual order are simultaneously undermined.[7]

General Traits of Open Text Films

In preparing for the analysis of *Weekend* as our representative Open Text film, however, we should look more closely at some general traits of the Open Text films. In contrast to the Closed Text film, there is a constant struggle or friction in an Open Text film between the story and its telling. A conventionally unified story with motivated character traits and continuous time and space no longer dominates the narrative, because these texts stress the presentation process itself. It was evident in discussion of *The Quiet Man* that classical films often produce a narrative discourse that presents the story but also tries to "fit" the style of the story being told. In these films, the story comes first and the role of the narrative discourse is to deliver that story clearly and concisely. In contrast, the Open Text films construct their story and narrative discourse in ways that call attention to the fact that they are two interdependent yet competing aspects of a narrative. In *Weekend*, for example, there are editing patterns that obscure even simple actions. Instead of an effort to keep the narrative discourse efficiently functional for the story, the narration becomes an active, highly visible manipulation, creating tension rather than unity.

The definition of the Open Text category as a sort of negation of more conventional narrative characteristics is no accident since the tendency of such films is to react against norms. One way to place the following discussion in perspective is to consider Francis Vanoye's notion of "dysnarration" as an Open Text strategy. According to Vanoye, dysnarration is "an operation of a *récit* [narrative] voluntarily challenging itself."[8] The goal of dysnarration, which Vanoye discusses specifically in relation to Robbe-Grillet's films, is indeed a negation, or breaking of the spectator's conventional illusions, such as the illusion that a film is a transparent reproduction of reality, or a "mirror onto the world."

Instead, dysnarration proposes three tactics: first, it reveals the arbitrariness of the concept of narrative in general; second, it underlines the usual simplicity of narrative films as opposed to the very concrete complexity of reality; and third, it makes the narrative's work on the signifiers more obvious, rather than naturalizing the signifier for the benefit of a clear and consistent signified.[9] We must keep in mind that these negative labels and characteristics—fragmenting, undercutting, contradicting—should be interpreted as productive and even parodic strategies rather than the failure to achieve more traditional results. As Vanoye writes, "Dysnarration replaces a finished product with elements of a product in the process of becoming. . . . It does tell new things, but in new ways."[10]

Within Open Text films, therefore, the story line is less resolved and the narrative discourse is more contradictory and heterogeneous. We can productively oppose its unresolved story to the linearity of the Closed Text's more complete story. This study has made frequent reference to the fact that the classical story is built up around segment-to-segment relations that help tie one event or sequence to the next, thereby maintaining a unified and cohesive story progression. But the stories in Open Text films like *Weekend* or Robbe-Grillet's *L'Homme qui ment* (*The Man Who Lies*, 1968) destroy, undercut, and parody the efficient segment-to-segment hooks that make classical stories so linear and coherent.

During the opening moments of *The Quiet Man*, Sean arrived in Ireland, he was driven toward Innisfree, then he was taken into a bar, and so forth. The beginning was constructed in concrete blocks of actions, one leading into the next. In *Weekend*, however, there are logical and temporal contradictions between the opening story events: Corinne tells her lover that she will not be riding to Oinville with Roland, then she is shown in the erotic monologue that is never anchored temporally or spatially within the diegesis, and next she *is* leaving for Oinville with Roland. Since the hermeneutic codes of Open Text films are not so clearly posed at the opening as they are in classical texts, the discontinuous story events disrupt any such direct story progression right from the start.

The first real characteristic of the Open Text film, therefore, is that the concept of narrative linearity is challenged on many levels at once. There is a similar example of a fragmented beginning in Robbe-Grillet's *The Man Who Lies*: The Trintignant character, Boris, dressed in a contemporary suit, is pursued through a forest and shot by the Nazis, then night falls and in the morning an apparently uninjured Boris wakes up and walks into town. Even the beginnings of these films fight against our understanding of where the story is heading since they break up the story events and provide inconsistent characters right from the start. Hence, the discontinuity of an Open Text film depends on temporal and spatial incongruities, as well as the fragmentation of story progression.

Thus, when identifying an Open Text film, one must first notice whether the story events are fragmented and confused rather than linear and unified. The story material is not pasted end-to-end in the Open Text film, so even trying to identify the order of diegetic events in a Godard or Robbe-Grillet film becomes a challenge. The subsequent labor of specifying which actions took place in which order is further complicated because these films question the very notion of a "taking place" or the possibility of there ever being a realistic setting. As Peter Brooks writes, "Readers learned to read the new novel, partly by abandoning certain expectations of coherence . . . and partly by learning to use the plot elements offered, in playful and fragmentary form."[11]

The second general trait of the Open Text's story construction, is that these stories are conventional, codified constructs dismissing any need for strict "plausibility." Conventions of plausibility typically struggle to naturalize their story production, until the result seems verisimilar and unproduced; as Seymour Chatman writes: "To naturalize a narrative convention means not only to understand it, but to 'forget' its conventional character."[12] However, plausibility, naturalization, and conventionalization are openly threatened by Open Text films that often verge on the absurd, or at least on the unmotivated fantastic, with actions defying both plausibility and efficiency. In Godard's *Weekend*, for instance, St. Just reads aloud to the camera, garbage workers recite Engels, and Corinne eats her husband; in *The Man Who Lies*, Boris can die and wake up again. The tight verisimilar codes so important to the Closed Text are severed and replaced by ellipses and contradictory events.

It should be obvious, however, that we need to find more concrete traits than fragmentation of the story line and an implausibility of actions, since all films could be argued to contain illogical actions and some degree of discontinuity. Thus the third characteristic builds upon the first two, while carrying them still further: The characters of Open Text films resemble those of the Open Story films in that they are incomplete and often lack any defined goals. Here, however, due to discontinuities in narration, the characters not only lack goals, they are also illogical in their actions. The diegetic world is composed of characters who often have obscure, even multiple personalities and wander about with vague or impossible goals, or no apparent purpose at all.

Many critics have called attention to the modernist shift away from the psychologically rounded, consistent characters of the realistic novel toward more complex characterizations. Modern psychology is often cited as a catalyst for the breakdown of the unified character. Gone are the linear characters of the nineteenth-century novel or classical film. Instead of uniform, directed characters, Open Text films feature complex collections of traits that cannot easily be fitted together into a centralized character function or role. Patricia Waugh writes that modernists play with the very notion of a fictional character being able to "go" anywhere: "The traditional fictional quest has thus been transformed into a quest for fictionality."[13] The lack of rounded, knowledgeable characters like *Weekend*'s Roland and Corinne, therefore, obscures the Open Text's story hermeneutics.

A fourth trait of the Open Text's story is the discontinuous time and space of the diegetic setting. Just as the characters are disunified collections of traits, the diegetic world is similarly disjointed since time and space are neither continuous nor linear. Instead of continuity and linearity, these stories produce a complex temporal and spatial world which cannot always be readily reconstructed or even followed by the spectator. If we begin with the time schemes, and break them into Genette's three divisions of duration, order, and frequency,[14] it becomes obvious that in an Open Text film the duration is fractured, order is confused and frequency of presentation of a single event often abstracts the overall temporal flow. For instance, Robbe-Grillet's films often manipulate these three components of temporal articulation. In *L'Immortelle*, there is a simple match-on-action cut where the character N turns in shot 191 to see what an old man is looking at. The match on N's turning, however, in shot 192, shows that he is wearing a different suit of clothes than in 191. Robbe-Grillet's disruption of costuming on the profilmic level challenges the diegesis because the temporal ellipsis in story time is not acknowledged by the conventional logic of a match-on-action.[15]

Throughout Robbe-Grillet's films, temporal incongruities abound on the larger levels, especially between scenes, since he uses temporal shifts like flashbacks, flash-forwards, and even dreams, without giving any coded cues about when these "inner" sequences begin or end. François Jost observes that story time for these modern films "is not just a point of departure, but rather a constant construction by the spectator."[16] Thus duration, order, and frequency here do not follow continuity rules and do not simply express the subjectivity of a specific character's point of view. Moreover, duration, order, and frequency of action do not necessarily clarify the events.

Spatial articulations are also discontinuous and fragmented in Open Text films. There are impossible spaces in these films, such as Roland's standing next to a poster and the previous scene's other characters during one shot in *Weekend* while he was just shown driving away from that same place in a preceding shot (see fig. 5.1). In *The Quiet Man*, Sean Thornton could never be in two places at the same time, but in a Godard or Robbe-Grillet film this is occasionally possible because a coherent space is not necessarily pertinent to the narration and space has become a mobile structure. In addition to blatantly impossible spatial arrangements, there are ambiguous spaces in these films where only fragments of a location are presented—fragments which do not seem to fit back together into a single concrete place. In *The Man Who Lies*, Boris runs through the woods, but he seems to be bounced great distances between shots. He is alternately close to and far from his pursuers, and later the entire forest will appear magically to be right next to a town that did not seem to be there before. Such discontinuity opens gaps in the story of the Open Text film thereby preserving the diegetic world's uncertainty.

Fig. 5.1. *Weekend.* Roland and gang by posters

These strategies of disruption make story comprehension a challenge and also make a complete story resolution impossible or unnecessary. When Chatman writes about Robbe-Grillet's fiction, he claims the novels have a *"story-manqué"*, since these tales fail to mention crucial events and leave huge gaps in character, time, space, and the logic of events.[17] Similarly, *L'Immortelle*'s fragmented story does not give the viewer the information necessary to reconstruct any stable diegesis. The Open Text's story, with its incomplete characters and ambiguous time and space, leaves the spectator with a collection of story fragments that cannot, or will not, be resolved by the end of the film.

As far as the narrative discourse is concerned, however, the two most important aspects of the Open Text's narration are its lack of secure closure and its dialogical point of view and narrative voice structures. These films look more like works in progress than conclusive framed texts. Openness here is a double process. On the one hand, it denotes the inconclusiveness of the film's ending, while on the other, it describes the openness of textual construction throughout the film. Thus a narrative discourse is open if it has a heterogeneous structure and a corresponding absence of narrative closure at the end.

On the level of narrative voice(s), there is a splintering of the textual narration. Umberto Eco, writing about openness in art, sees conventional art works as "univocal," because they communicate a directed authorial message. On the other hand, more modern texts work toward a "plurivocal" message that combines fiction with the rhetoric and prepared messages of diverse "non-artistic" sources.[18] By using a composite or collage of literary, historic, and cultural messages, the modern text expands and challenges the idea of authorship. The concept of a single author creating a monological or authoritatively unified narrative discourse is undermined and thrown into doubt by these collective and dialogical narrative strategies.

The Quiet Man's epilogue returned to the point of view of a primary narrator superior to the internal narration of Father Lonergan. In the Open Text it is more difficult to posit a single narrative voice at work, unless the narrator is posited as a playful, contradictory composer of the film, as David Bordwell has done.[19] But whether one lumps many heterological voices together under the banner of a single, bricoleur narrator, or sticks to discussing the narrative discourse as one which employs many distinct voices, the point of view structures in these films remain complex and multiple as they compose the narration. *Weekend*, for instance, uses a variety of intertitles, interior monologues, and elliptical editing patterns. The narrative discourse is a collection of musical interventions, intertitles, and editing styles which all lead to a decentered or fragmented telling of an elliptical story.

The heterological narration of the Open Text also accords with the idea of dialogic narration as developed by Mikhail Bakhtin. For Bakhtin, the dialogical text is one in which "the individual voice cannot make itself heard except by its integration with the complex chorus of other, already present voices."[20] If a modern art work is seen as a collection of voices, which in the cinema will include music, sound, editing logic as well as interior monologues or secondary narrators, then each voice is part of the text's acknowledgment of the multiple sources and functions of language systems in society. In modern literature, Bakhtin writes, there is "a social plurilinguism which penetrates an art work and then stratifies its language."[21] The modern film, like a James Joyce or John Dos Passos novel, may build a heterogeneous narration for itself which takes advantage of the multiplicity of social language systems.

Examples of dialogical narration's importance to Open Text films will be developed in detail later in this chapter, but for the moment we need only recall the disrupted match-on-action in *L'Immortelle*. Because the character's clothes change between shots of the match there is a gap in time that threatens the story. In addition, there is also a contradiction on the level of the narrative discourse that produces that gap. Historically, the match-on-action was developed to unify the discontinuous time of filming, so changing one index of continuity, the actor's clothes, forces a contradiction of the editing voice that set up the match in the first place. Thus, the disruption produced by the change of clothes challenges the production of the edited sequence which is trying to establish unity.

If permanent contradictions in the narration of a film are not explained by the end, they become permanent gaps that force disruptions in the discourse. Determining whether a film is an Open Text, therefore, must take into account both the level of textual construction (testing the narrative discourse for its degree of unity), and the inconclusiveness of the ending itself. With such a splintered, contradictory telling of the Open Text film, lack of closure becomes a necessary condition. There is no longer a termination effect produced by closure devices, so in place of any unified, harmonic narrative, a productive tension pervades the text.

Since the Open Text films have gone against the dominant forms, these films will not be able to use a conventional closure device to frame their narration. The musical themes will not be woven into a final reprise, the diegetic world will not be clearly suspended by a freeze-frame, and the point of view cannot simply shift back to the untroubled control of a primary, organizing narrator. Iouri Lotman writes that contemporary narratives play with the notions of beginning and ending to such an extent that they can often be said to have "anti-beginnings."[22] But if they have anti-beginnings, they can also have anti-endings, meaning that these films work against establishing a secure unified termination effect, since to attach a solid ending that explained the loose structure of the film would undermine the text's own construction and the openness it had achieved up to that point, or appear outrageously parodic at the very least.

One of Bakhtin's recurring arguments surrounding the value of the dialogical text is that these texts exploit the diversity of cultural discourses, thereby preserving a multiplicity of languages within narrative itself. Since all tales are intertextual, the dialogical text opens up connections between texts, moving away from the artificial and naive limits of monological narratives. A dialogical film's ending will not allow it to be packaged and conclusive, but instead the ending keeps making connections with other, equally active forms of social communication.[23] According to Bakhtin, conventional stylistic critics, "enclose all stylistic phenomena within the monological context of the closed context."[24] A truly open film will open up the very idea of "text" by its use of a variety of heterogeneous narrative tactics, hence no single strategy or level will be able to close off the film at the end.

The language systems in *Weekend* remain intertextual and stratified at the end as well as during the narration. As Guy Scarpetta writes of Godard, "for him it is not the 'representation' that must be challenged, but the code."[25] By breaking the codes of monological, closed readings he produces truly Open Text films. Godard has a collage style and proceeds by working from what he calls "bits and pieces."[26] Moreover, Godard's films struggle to maintain a loose bricoleur style in order to force the texts to remain multiple and heterogeneous, especially in their endings. Seeing that the final action of *Weekend* is to spell out its *Numéro de Contrôle* in order to refer to the institutional and industrial processes of production, is therefore central to understanding the labor of a dialogical narrative.

Similarly, during the final shot of *Sauve qui peut (la vie)* (1980) the Godard character's ex-wife and daughter walk down an alley, and pass a small orchestra playing the film's theme music. But the actors do not suddenly fall out of character, as they do at the end of *Blazing Saddles* (Brooks, 1974) or *Stardust Memories* (Allen, 1980). Instead they continue acting. Rather than *Sauve qui peut* having a final shot that says only that "this was all just a movie," there is the revelation of the orchestra while the two characters disappear back into what is now both a fictional and real world. The narrative does not simply end with the display of the profilmic process, instead there is a combination of tactics that both reveal and continue the fictionality, with neither level proving dominant. The fiction and its telling share the last shot, and this duality serves as an illustration of Bakhtin's concept of the dialogical.

Films by Godard and Robbe-Grillet routinely produce new forms that challenge conventions of structure and evade traditional closure. Godard films in particular offer a rich place for analysis since they often test the very definitions of narrative while struggling against notions of closure. *Weekend*, with its fragmented narrative line, diverse intertitles, impossible characters, and political monologues, looks like a muddle of film modes and genres, not all of which fit easily within a unified concept of "the fiction film."

The Unresolved Story and *Weekend*

Upon its release, *Weekend* was cited in a *Positif* review as an interesting mixture of genres that resembled dream-like poetry more than narrative cinema. According to that review, the characters were very obvious in being incongruous with each other and the diegesis as a whole. But this stylistic mixture and the resulting complexity proved too unsettling for many of *Weekend*'s contemporary critics, and *Positif*'s reviewer complained the film was too disunified and was "a film found in the toilet," as well as in the cosmos.[27] Yet it is precisely this confusing and heterogeneous structure that sets *Weekend* up as one of the more appropriate Godard films to be analyzed for its Open Text qualities.

The ending of *Weekend*, (segment 25), begins on the intertitle *Vendé Miaire* (the Republican calendar's first month) in shot 215, then shot 216 is an extreme close-up of FLSO leader Kalfon's jacket sleeve and clutched hand. As the shot continues, Kalfon says, "When your foot slips on a frog you feel disgust. But brush against the human body and the skin of your fingers splits." He then opens his hand to reveal a tiny frog. Corinne, in voice-off, says only, "Ah, bon." Then shot 217 is a medium-long shot of Kalfon and Corinne at the left, with the blood-spattered Ernest cooking at the right. Kalfon continues his pompous monologue by comparing the beating heart of a dead shark to the fact that a person's intestines continue to move long after he or she has had sex.

Corinne, still in the medium-long shot, asks Kalfon why the two situations are comparable, and he replies, "Because man sees the horror of his fellow-man." Kalfon proclaims that he has never discovered a worse malady than meditating upon the strangeness of the human being. Then he calls to the cook Ernest who approaches and dishes up food for each of them. Next, (shot 218) there is a close-up of Corinne, filmed straight-on, eating (see fig. 5.2). In voice-off, Kalfon tells her she is eating a mixture of roast pork and some of the remains of the British tourists. Corinne looks off-screen left toward Kalfon, but only asks, "The ones with the Rolls?" By way of an answer, Kalfon adds that there is a bit of her husband in it also. With no emotional reaction, Corinne turns to look off-right and says, "After this Ernest, I'll have another piece." The shot fades and the end-titles of "Fin du Conte" and "Fin du Cinéma" appear (see fig. 5.3), then turn into the *visa de contrôle* certification number.

While this ending does at least answer any questions about what happened to Roland (who had last been seen bleeding on a road), it still leaves the story unresolved on many levels. The analysis of *Weekend*'s story, therefore, looks at the film's failure to use linear, segment-to-segment structures, its dismissal of conventions of plausibility, its inconsistent characters, and discontinuous time and space. One story element that allows us to consider all these aspects of story construction is *Weekend*'s use of character. Roland and Corinne are not unlike many other Godard characters; in fact they resemble *Pierrot le fou*'s (1965) Ferdinand and Marianne, as well as *Made in USA*'s (1966) Paula Nelson. But they are not as verbal or reflexive as *Tout va bien*'s Jacques and Susan. In *Tout va bien*, the couple can explain their own pasts, with Jacques even providing images to illustrate his memories. Jacques also has the insight that as a couple they are "no longer moving at the same speed," which is the type of remark more typical of a classical film character.

In contrast, both Roland and Corinne are less developed and thus closer to bundles of character traits than self-conscious individuals. Unlike many art films, however, *Weekend*'s story does begin by establishing the two main characters and their goals. Whereas, ironically, in *The 400 Blows* it was difficult to know what Antoine wanted, Godard's *Weekend* opens with a conventional telephone conversation to let Ro-

Fig. 5.2. Corinne eats Roland

Fig. 5.3. Fin de Cinéma title

land define his own immediate quest. Corinne has a parallel conversation with a man on the balcony outlining precisely what she plans to do.

In this opening scene, Corinne tells her lover that she made certain Roland did not fix the car's brakes, and that she hopes he dies in an accident. She also says that she plans to ride with someone else so as to avoid getting caught in an accident of her own making. Meanwhile, Roland is simultaneously talking to his mistress on the telephone, so we find out that he has also been trying to kill Corinne for a long time. In addition, Roland explains to his girlfriend that "the important thing is for Corinne's old man to croak. Afterwards, when Corinne's got the money, we'll deal with her."

These opening conversations set up the initial action code of the film: Roland and Corinne will go separately to her parents' house to make sure the dying father will leave them some money. Moreover, deadlines are set up for the action: The mother expects them by lunch time, and Roland has told his mistress he will be back by Monday. Admittedly, these characters' explanations are still slightly incomplete, and they parody the efficient openings of a classical text since the spectator is not told who these diegetic narratees (the man on the balcony and woman on the phone) actually are. Furthermore, the conversations are somewhat fragmented and become too hurried to deliver all the information—it is difficult to catch the fact that Roland is going to take the parents home from the hospital and that Corinne's ultimate hope is that those three all die in an accident. The actual financial arrangement surrounding the dying father is never made clear either. We are not sure whether the dying man has a will, or whether they hope to convince him to change it at the last minute to obtain the mother's share.

Thus, from the beginning Corinne and Roland are set up as two farcical potential murderers, each plotting the death of the other. Comically, these motifs of homicidal plotting and deceit are the only two character traits to remain consistent throughout the film. Later, when the two are forced to walk to her parents' house in Oinville, they become fearful that they may arrive too late and the mother will get all the money. Roland comforts Corinne by saying, "We'll just torture her to change her mind."

These scenes of Roland and Corinne threatening everyone around them build steadily throughout the film. In scene 3, Roland and Corinne dent the neighbor's car and spraypaint the woman's designer dress.

Later, Roland chases other cars off the road, and after their own accident he allows Corinne to be raped in the ditch by a passerby. The two most violent acts committed by the pair, the murders of Emily Bronte and Corinne's mother, are thus consistent with the established character traits; these events also prepare the spectator for Corinne's being able to eat Roland by the end.

So why, if it is somewhat consistent with *Weekend*'s story logic that Corinne devour her husband, is the final scene inadequate to resolve Corinne's characterization? The problem is that while Corinne's hatred for her husband remains constant to the end, many other traits have been dropped by the wayside as the story advanced. By simply outlining several of her character functions we can find strong differences between Corinne and the more conventional characters of Mary Kate Danaher, Antoine Doinel, and *Tout va bien*'s Jacques in the preceding three categories.

Corinne begins as dishonest and materialistic. She wants the money for herself and, like Roland, she sees the world as consumer products and brand names. Corinne's screaming for her designer handbag after their car accident is exemplary. Yet by the end of the film Corinne has forsaken society, apparently abandoning the world of inheritance and designer clothes, and is the new mate of FLSO leader Kalfon. She no longer even mentions the money which was the original reason for their drive to the country. She has lept from being "une petite bourgeoise" to living as a cannibalistic revolutionary.

Corinne's varied activities support Bordwell's claim that Godard characters are often "presented as a sketchy construct, a precipitate out of the mixture of narrational modes."[28] Corinne fills the role of a typical art film character when she describes her sexual fantasy in silhouette in scene 2 (see fig. 5.4), but she is a character out of a "B" western during the Arizona Jules sequence, and then she becomes an allegorical guerrilla-theater character at the end when she eats Roland. It is precisely Corinne's final act of the film which troubles Robin Wood so much because it does not fit with the tone of many of her earlier actions. He writes that "she enjoys eating him, not in any spirit of symbolic possessiveness, but simply as a tasty bit of meat."[29] Her final actions, therefore, do not complete any strict character development or explain her earlier behavior throughout the film, and they do not even supply us with her thoughts about eating Roland.

Corinne's characterization shifts and meanders like the course of *Weekend*'s story line. The strange beginning, with its bits of outra-

Fig. 5.4. Corinne's erotic monologue

geous character behavior and blunt dialogue, sets up a false impression of the actions which will follow. The film will not center on the relationships between Corinne, Roland, and their lovers; instead the story will revolve around the disruption of the expected journey. There will be a car accident, but Corinne is in the car with Roland after saying she would not ride with him; we never hear from the two lovers again; and we never find out the fate of the inheritance by the end of the film. *Weekend* has gone beyond the ironic twists of films like *Bande à part* (1964), where the end simply parodies a tacked-on happy ending. Here the money is lost in the story and is apparently even forgotten by Corinne.

The development of characters is even more problematic in *Weekend*'s use of oneiric and impossible characters. Saint-Just, Gros Pouce, and Joseph Balsamo appear only in isolated scenes, and they seem to have no collective function other than to interrupt Roland and Corinne's journey. While their insertion into the story does achieve both comic and political effects, none of these characters is ever referred to again by Roland and Corinne, so their status is left open. Characters serve a plurality of functions, none of which are resolved by the ending—no one awakes out of a sound sleep surrounded by book jackets that evoke all these fictional worlds. We never know to whom Corinne told her erotic tale, whether Joseph Balsamo was a subjective fantasy, or what movie the Italian actors from a co-production are working on. Furthermore, the double appearance of Jean-Pierre Léaud as both the St. Just figure (recalling his performance in *La Chinoise* in the same costume) and as the love-sick man singing in the phone booth, continues this play of characters who seem to exist at several competing levels of the fiction.

When speaking about his own films, Godard stresses the way his characters struggle against the heavily coded conventions of both character and verisimilitude. In an *Art Press* interview, Godard cites an example of how one can fight against these conventions: "Today one codes. . . . If it is the admiral who says, 'The battleship must leave at five o'clock,' that is fine because he has a helmet on. But if we never saw who was speaking about the battleship and if he was dressed as Davy Crockett, they would say: 'Alright now, is he admiral or a trapper? What does this mean?'"[30]

It is precisely this sort of play with character that *Weekend* invokes by Léaud portraying two different characters. The viewer is forced to ask, "Is he St. Just or a spurned lover?" Often characters cannot easily be placed within the story since their functions are not immediately evident, and the result is that their signification remains loose, multiple, and open.

Toby Mussman, writing about the apparent disorder of a Godard film's diegetic world, claims that, "often at the first viewing of a Godard film we find ourselves wondering just where the central story is."[31] In *Weekend*, the excessive characters act collectively as asides or disruptions that distract Roland and Corinne and pull the spectator's attention away from the immediate narrative progression. It is Godard's working against simple codification that also allows him to link his characters to extratextual events (Roland has to answer political questions like "Would you rather sleep with Mao or LBJ?" before he can hitch a ride), or connect them to other artistic references (such as Roland's lighting Emily Bronte's dress on fire) (see fig. 5.5). It is not enough to watch Roland and Corinne travel to Oinville, but the narrator also seems intrigued by whether they prefer LBJ or Mao. The audience begins its own work during all this by asking "What is pertinent here?" and "Where is the central story?"

Open Text films, therefore, challenge the status of basic character traits, while they undercut key story events and actions. In *Weekend*, like

Fig. 5.5. "Mao or LBJ?"

Godard's *Alphaville* (1965) or *Made in USA*, there is a sort of central motivating action code since the characters are searching for something specific (here the inheritance). But Roland and Corinne's journey is a collection of pieces of a trip, and its linearity is constantly disrupted. Hence, while there is always a minimal action code, it is the stylistic play as well as the insertion of these excessive characters that interferes with the minimal central journey in *Weekend*'s story.

As mentioned, Open Text films are fragmented rather than linear, and that the characters and their actions exceed the usual plausibility of the verisimilar. *Weekend* is composed of strange parenthetical scenes that interrupt the already loose action code "driving to Oinville," and every event becomes more autonomous than those in a more classical or homogeneous film. One way that other modern texts, such as Fellini's *8 1/2*, employ similar disjointed or implausible actions, is to frame the film with a controlling subjective point of view. But while Guido's fantasies and his proposed film script are read as motivating the complexity and improbabilities of *8 1/2*, *Weekend* does not offer any such primary intradiegetic narrating source. *Weekend*, like Robbe-Grillet's *The Man Who Lies*, never provides a primary narrative situation that clarifies which scenes were "true" or subjective in relation to the other scenes. In Open Text films there is not the security of absolute or objective scenes from which to position or understand the other scenes since all sequences are equally suspect and fictional.

In *Weekend*, there is no privileged character, no individual who is more plausible than the others, and no fictional "reality" vs. "subjectivity" in the story. In addition, no events seem to create others, so there is no motivation to decide whether Joseph Balsamo was or was not present. The film's competing narrative strategies make Roland's burning of Emily Bronte no less plausible than his being hijacked by Balsamo, son of God and Dumas.[32] A film built so heavily on metaphor and intertextual reference opens its diegetic boundaries to include a wide variety of events and characters.

But this loose construction, which inserts what Bordwell has called "competing narrative modes" within a single film, does more than create the absurd and comic violence that Robin Wood mentions.[33] *Weekend*'s narrative strategy presents the spectator with a dialogic pattern of event-to-event connections. In writing about similar literary texts, Julia Kristeva has outlined the polymorphous quality of these narrative systems that go beyond simple cause-and-effect ordering, or that deny the possibility to "prove and verify" a narrative's events and time scheme. According to Kristeva, "A truly polymorphous text defies the establishment of a systematic, constructive process to determine whether or not a sequence of the text is plausible."[34] Kristeva adds that the plausible remains outside the polymorphous text, since plausible texts are finished products and thus easily consumed by the spectating public.

Similarly, the characters, actions and events of *Weekend*'s story are all denied a strict plausibility since no single ordering principle selects who and what is in this film. If St. Just can be here, why not include Robespierre? Where is Chateaubriand since we have a Bronte? The loose journey structure prepares the viewer for these encounters, but the spectator does not get enough clues to begin truly playing the game and guessing what comes next in this film. Within and between *Weekend*'s scenes, the story construction actively challenges the spectator's comprehension and second-guessing of the plot and story. Marie-Claire Ropars-Wuilleumier writes that Godard has often refused "to accept any established narrative syntax, which would have been founded on a conventional respect of the visual continuity."[35] This rejection of a plausible and continuous visual diegesis makes the film avoid building toward any "more probable" choices, and makes a unified and resolved story impossible.

The segment-to-segment ordering of the story events becomes less strict as the film progresses, and the existence of interruptions or disruptions by entire scenes loosens *Weekend*'s story construction until it becomes more and more disjointed. The coherence of the text is not simply dependent upon the sequential arrangement of story elements, since the efficient scene-to-scene hooks of the classical text are now removed or obscured. Bordwell describes this disjunctive structure in Godard films as a "spatialization of the syuzhet" and writes that, "The chief effect is to fragment the process of viewing into a series of discrete moments."[36] The spectator in this narrative model follows several of the more continuous strands of action (perhaps the most concrete moments of Roland and Corinne's journey to the mother's house.) But the spectator simultaneously minimizes or even forgets the excessive scenes and details which do not complement that primary strand, as s/he judges these scenes to be of secondary importance. Thus, the "Musical Action" recital at the farmhouse, or Léaud's singing phone call may be repressed or ignored by the spectator since these autonomous scenes do not immediately advance the basic thrust of the story action. An extreme and manifest example of this minimizing of the secondary events is Pauline Kael's review of *Weekend* urging the audience to go out and buy popcorn when the garbage workers begin their dialogue (see fig. 5.6).

This paratactic or spatialized narrative strategy changes the spectator's role and reduces the possibility of story resolution. *Weekend*'s story, therefore, with its open qualities, its competing lines of action, and its constant yet erratic interruptions, could continue indefinitely. Earlier we saw that some paratactic structures are cyclical or determined by some external form, such as the days of the week in *Mr. Hulot's Holiday*. But the Open Text film *Weekend* shares only the idea of interchangeable day scenes with these strict paratactic films, while it has even less of an inscribed termination point. The film does not end on Monday as its title suggests it could.

Weekend's story construction fits Kristeva's observation that modern, productive, dialogical texts proceed more by "rays" of action than by linear connections.[37] Thus a scene incorporating St. Just's monologue switches the action from "Roland and Corinne walking to Oinville," to "the discourse of St. Just." Roland and Corinne just happen to walk past him, and then they move literally from the foreground to the back-

Fig. 5.6. African garbage worker

ground; as they keep walking their own words are gradually drowned out by St. Just. In many scenes the story action detours along these tangential rays in order to emphasize secondary events like the piano playing in the "Musical Action," the garbage workers' dialogue, or the slaughter of animals, instead of concentrating on the actual journey.

The effect of all this disruption on the story's progression, which certainly comes as much from ellipses as from the veering off on interruptive and excessive plot tangents, is to produce a double challenge for the spectator. Godard's Open Text story construction has the doubly contradictory function of distancing and actively engaging the spectator. The viewers are slowed down so they find themselves trying to locate the central story in this assault of seemingly excessive story fragments. This frustration demands a more active spectating process. When spectators do not know where a film is headed they tend to watch everything (or nothing) because there is no way to be sure which elements will prove "significant" later on. In *Weekend*, for instance, the kinds of repetitions from scene to scene are unusual. For the scene of Corinne's fantasy monologue what will recur will be the mixture of sexual taboos and food rather than the man involved. (The egg mentioned in the fantasy will become more important as a motif than any other element.)

As spectators we not only fail to guess "what will come next," but also find it difficult to know what was important about such scenes as the one showing the sports car crashing into the tractor. Is the most central element the idea of exploited farmers, the car's Chrysler engine, the battle between the classes, the common bond of anti-Semitism, or simply the blood pouring down the windshield? A spectator at an Open Text film must watch, weigh, and criticize every aspect of the text. *Weekend*'s spectator cannot be an uncritical movie consumer, but rather becomes an active film critic, both distanced and engaged by the Open Text story's "bits and pieces." The films shift direction constantly; *Weekend* sets up strong patterns and then changes them before the viewer gets comfortable or completely competent with the story's code systems.

The dynamism of the classical text is partially derived from the spectator trying to refer to both past film experience and the patterns of the film being watched in order to anticipate the ending before it is revealed. But in the Open Text film, the process of viewing and second-guessing the end is necessarily much different. Open Text spectators must assimilate shifts in character and story by stockpiling a memory of potentially significant motifs for the time when the film ends, hoping the conclusion will then give some justification to the story's selection and combination of elements. In *Weekend*, however, the end will not help place all the story events into an easily consumable order since very potential for a termination effect has been reduced by the loose story continuity. Here the ending does not resolve or justify all the twists and turns of the story's events. It is worth quoting part of one review by Claude Greenberg from *Film et Vie* that illustrates the confusion left by a truly unresolved ending:

> Finally, the last reel finishes with the words, "End of Tale, End of Cinema." At last here are some reference points. Are they the keys? Hardly at all it seems. The final words of Ghelderode's play *Sortie de l'acteur* were "What is the key to the mystery"—"The mystery has no door." Going even further, if we may paraphrase, this cinema has no lock. (It is always by largely open portals that we enter onto the baroque path of an epic.)[38]

Point of View and Intertextual Reference

Our discussion of irresolution in *Weekend*'s story has already referred to some of the film's discursive activities. Now those strategies can be studied more closely as we analyze its heterogeneous narration, which can be identified by a lack of closure devices, as well as loose narrative construction throughout. In his work on textual openness, Eco emphasizes this second level: "This sort of opening of the second degree, to which contemporary art aspires, could be defined in terms of *signification*, as the interweaving and multiplication of the possible meanings of the message."[39] Both these levels of textual openness will be considered in this section.

Weekend has a narrative discourse that must be discussed in terms of its point of view and narrative voice structures. The competition between its intertitles, interior monologues, elliptical editing patterns, and musical interventions all help fragment and eventually open up the narration of this Open Text film. By contrast, the films of the other three categories followed definite patterns of focalization. *The Quiet Man*, for instance, had two narrators, one inside and the other outside the diegesis, but both telling the story of Sean Thornton. These narrators made certain that even when Sean was not physically present in a scene all the action was directly related to him. Similarly, in *The 400 Blows*, all the scenes were tied to Antoine.

But *Weekend* has discarded this efficient focalization process. The narrative discourse does not limit itself to what physically surrounds Roland and Corinne nor to what relates only to their journey. On the level of point of view, the film begins by staying close to Roland and Corinne's knowledge—we hear each of them outline their plans in the initial scene—but soon more ambiguity develops, and the focalization wanders so that the spectator can no longer place certain scenes in relation to the two protagonists.

Corinne's sexual monologue with the unidentified man challenges the spectator's activity since there is no way to decide when this scene took place, who she was with, or even whether she was telling the truth. The conditions of this scene cannot be tested and it is as if more is being denied than revealed by the narrative discourse. There is not enough light on the backlit man's face to identify him, and there is not a reverse-shot to show us whether she is in an office, hotel, or apartment. Thus, *Weekend*'s second segment presents us with a nine-and-a-half minute narrative instance, the context for which is denied.

As the film progresses there are more and more examples of events which are not specifically related to Roland and Corinne's journey. By *Weekend*'s final three segments, the focalization is even more dispersed. During the entire FLSO section the audience has witnessed many scenes that are never linked temporally or spatially to Roland and Corinne's actual presence. A pig and goose are slaughtered, a young woman is painted, and the whole FLSO troop looks out onto the pond as Kalfon preaches Lautréamont's "Ancient Sea" monologue in voice-off (see fig. 5.7). This final section concerns the FLSO collective, yet occasionally singles out Kalfon, his dying girlfriend, or Ernest the cook, in close-up. But there is no longer any strict adherence to showing only what the central characters experience or witness. Even Roland's death occurs in the off-screen space, as if he were simply another kidnapped tourist rather than the male lead of the film.

While the narrating discourse in *The 400 Blows* narrowed the focalization at the end to help close off the point of view structures, *Weekend* splinters the focalization from beginning to end. The final shots of Kalfon, Ernest, and Corinne involve a casual conversation about the horror of man, and then the cut-in to Corinne eating Roland. The final shot only retrospectively finishes the scene, and in no way acts as the culmination of a return to Corinne as the focalized center of the film. In *The 400 Blows*, there is a systematic limiting of the point of view to parallel Antoine's isolation, yet in *Weekend*, the close-up gives a detail,

Fig. 5.7. FLSO members paint a woman's body

but does not finish any movement toward a single point of view structure or focalizing system.

One of the related traits of narrative discourse in an Open Text is the "plurivocal" quality created by the competition between narrative voices. By using a sort of collage style, which is never tied together or unified by a primary narrator, the Open Text film presents itself as a network of narrative voices which challenge rather than reinforce one another. In *Weekend*, intertitles contradict the image and soundtrack, and there are elliptical editing patterns that break up the events they represent. All these tactics lead to the sort of bricoleur narration that marks an Open Text film.

By taking a brief look at *Weekend*'s intertitles we can see their wide variety of functions. In his article on Godard, Guy Scarpetta mentions Godard's tactic of "literalization of the spectacle," in the form of intertitles and writing, to address the spectator directly. This literalization undercuts the illusion of representation, reminds the audience they are watching a film, and denaturalizes the spectacle by including extratextual allusions and citations.[40] These titles open up the text since they not only refer to extratextual references, yet rarely appear to dominate or determine the scenes they interrupt. A simple intertitle such as "2:00," for example, cannot necessarily be read as an objective fact.

Beginning with a concrete example from *Weekend* will both help explain the concept of competing voices and illustrate Godard's particular use of intertitles. The temporal unity of scene 4, the traffic jam, is violated by the editing pattern that repeats and overlaps the action, but it is even more noticeably disrupted by the intertitles which pretend to clarify the time of the event. The shot, during which the camera moves parallel to the traffic jam, could last eight minutes without interruption, but instead it is intercut with the titles "Weekend", "Saturday 11 o'clock," "1:40," and "2:00." A tracking shot is generally used to follow characters continually through time and space, yet here the titles contradict the visible time of the shot. The viewer is left to decide whether the time indicated by the titles, from 11:00 to 2:10, has indeed passed, or whether the time of the image, roughly eight minutes, is correct. It is a contradiction which the film creates but does not resolve (see figs. 5.8 and 5.9).

The interjection of other, less concrete intertitles works very differently in *Weekend* than does the immediate contradiction of the three hours vs. eight minutes of scene 4. These other intertitles come from such a variety of historical or fictional realms that they have a double

Fig. 5.8. Traffic jam

Fig. 5.9. 1:40

function of first, collectively interrupting scenes, but then secondly, on an individual case-by-case basis they lend depth to the narration. Their common characteristic is that they disrupt the image and sound with written language (and all with the same print-face and red, white, and/or blue colors), yet individually they refer to a wide variety of extratextual concepts.

One such intervention is the use of intertitles of the names of some months in the French Revolutionary calendar. These titles come during the final FLSO section of the film, and have the immediate effect of linking the modern-day revolutionaries to the original Revolution. They also imply that the FLSO exists on a different time scheme than does the rest of the diegetic world, since the film's more concrete time-titles of "11:00" or "Saturday" have now disappeared. Yet the reason that the month Pluvoise falls where it does in the film while Vendé Miaire, the first Republican month, is the last one mentioned in the film, is all left unclear. Kalfon never refers to these names of the months, so they are never tied to the diegesis that they interrupt. They act as an intrusive voice which is potentially significant, but which has only tangential ties with the surrounding images and sounds.

Other titles act intertexually to refer to diverse fictional, artistic or pop culture traditions. During the FLSO gun fight, for instance, in which Corinne is nearly exchanged for another woman, the intertitle "Arizona Jules" is used. This sort of fictional reference to both the Arizona Jim of Renoir's *Le Crime de M. Lange* (1935), and Truffaut's *Jules and Jim* (1961), is typical of *Weekend*'s titles. Here Godard is expecting the spectator to be familiar enough with both films to be able to identify the condensation of Arizona Jim with Jules and Jim.

In addition to identifying the films referred to by the Arizona Jules title, the audience also has to continue making the title meaningful by remembering that Lange's Arizona Jim knew nothing about the real West and could only play at recreating its myths and stereotypes. Thus an additional way to read the shoot-out in *Weekend* would posit the FLSO's game of cowboys in a modern setting is just as infantile as M. Lange was in his fantasies about the West. Godard's reference to *Jules and Jim* remains more obscure, referring in part to the struggle between two male friends (here embodied in the two rival revolutionary camps instead of a German and Frenchman) over a woman. This single in-tertitle, therefore, calls up many potential meanings, the full significance of which depends on the resourcefulness, background, and patience of the spectator. These titles interrupt and open up the text by forcing the

161

spectator to consider whether Roland and Kalfon are in any way like Jules and Jim; whether Kalfon is a "just" criminal like M. Lange; and whether Truffaut's Catherine has anything in common with Godard's Corinne.

The intertitles in *Weekend* challenge the image and soundtracks in the traffic jam example, and break the flow of the story line in the other examples. Some titles, like "Light in August" are even more obscure, referring to Faulkner's novel of the same name, and perhaps to other more distant texts or events as well, such as Gremillon's *Lumiere d'ete* (1943). These intertitles communicate on a level that contradicts or at the very least distracts from the story events being told. Time itself is determined by various strategies that use metaphoric ("A Tuesday in the Hundred Year's War"), precise ("1:40"), and figurative ("Pluvoise") designations that result in a multiplicity of techniques for labeling *Weekend*'s temporality. The changing methods of representing time require the spectator to posit several narrating tactics or voices that refuse to build a unified or homogeneous *énoncé*. Even the film's open "Weekend" title sets up the playfulness of titles since it repeats the word over and over, suggesting that this weekend may be endless (see fig. 5.10).

The intertextual references within *Weekend*'s intertitles, character names, and other textual indices to such figures as Lewis Carroll, Sergei Eisenstein, Bertolt Brecht/Brigitte Bardot, and Honoré de Balzac, open up the film to a broad realm of cultural texts. Some of these references are beyond the background of even the most academic of spectators. Intertextual references in general, according to Laurent Jenny, create paradigmatic interruptions, "introducing a new way of reading which destroys the linearity of the text."[41] These intertextual breaks of the linear flow of the narrative also fit Eco's claim that one tactic of openness available to a text involves requiring extraordinary extratextual labor by the spectator. "The 'openness' becomes an instrument for revolutionary pedagogy," according to Eco, since it challenges both codes of fiction and of spectatorship.[42]

The broad field of reference required of the spectator, combined with the mixture of styles of presentation and multiple narrative voices, signals an Open Text film. Eco describes this sort of experimental openness, which is similar to Joyce's novels, as "aesthetically organizing *a referential apparatus which is already, by itself, open and ambiguous.*"[43] By preventing immediate comprehension, *Weekend*'s intertitles force a wedge between the time of viewing and the time of understanding. Some titles may only be understood after the screening, or even during subsequent research and a second or third viewing of the film.

Fig. 5.10. Opening title (Red, White, & Blue)

Because *Weekend*'s titles cannot be privileged as any more correct than the other elements within the scenes they interrupt, and because the titles are never anchored within the narrative discourse, they remain autonomous statements in this already heterogeneous film. This collection of intertitles is close to the definition of dialogical discourse since they set one language system against another. They allow the written words to contradict the images and sounds surrounding them. Patricia Waugh describes similar texts: "The conflict of languages and voices is apparently resolved in realistic fiction through their subordination to the dominant 'voice' of the omniscient, godlike author. Novels which Bakhtin refers to as 'dialogic' resist such resolution. Metafiction *displays* and *rejoices in* the impossibility of such a resolution."[44] Similarly, *Weekend* resists resolving how much time has passed during the traffic jam and does not give a single key for the spectator to read all the film's intertitles in relation to the actions that they disrupt.

Conflicting Narrative Voices

These sorts of contradictions between different language systems within a film, here written vs. audio-visual, resemble characteristics of

163

Bakhtin's concept of the dialogical text. In his *Esthétique et théorie du roman*, Bakhtin writes that every fictional work is a collection of social languages and therefore becomes a system of narrative languages.[45] More conventional texts try to repress their multiplicity by asserting a dominant, orchestrating voice to control the various languages, but Open Texts like *Weekend* foreground the competition of voices, remaining overtly dialogic. According to Bakhtin, the real job of stylistic analysis is to discover all the languages that comprise the text, "the degree of separation between each of the languages, and the ultimate semantic stand of the work."[46]

The ultimate semantic stand of *Weekend*, therefore, with intertitles undercutting fictional continuity, is to break the codes of monologic narration. In an interview, Godard speaks of the audience's hesitation to follow multiple messages: "People nowadays. . . . They are not disoriented by advertising, for example. . . . In four seconds they see Ajax, a carriage, Marlboro—they don't say: 'Marlboro, that has nothing to do with the rest,'—they follow very well, and me too. . . . And yet, if they see that in a film. . . . They don't follow it."[47] Similarly, Godard's use of conflicting voices in the form of excessive and disruptive intertitles expands the realm of the cinematic and helps motivate a new, more productive spectator. This tendency to make the cinema more densely communicative and, in effect, dialogic, is reinforced by Godard's statement that what is important "is not the destruction of the cinema, but the destruction of its forms."[48]

Another strategy for breaking with conventional cinema's forms of narrative discourse and spectatorship is to use elliptical editing to force major contradictions in the spatial and temporal articulation of the story events. Two key scenes, Joseph Balsamo's appearance, and the car crash, can illustrate the competition of narrative voices between the actual editing pattern or ordering of details, and the diegetic events portrayed.

In the end of scene 6, Roland and Corinne are driving with their convertible top down. In shot 54, the odometer intertitle reads 9528.0 Km. In shot 55, Corinne asks Roland whether it might rain, and Roland replies, "Don't annoy me. I said it's going to rain," while intertitle shot 56 proclaims that it is Saturday at 5 o'clock. But in shot 57, they stop to pick up Mary Madeleine in the rain (but while Roland checks out her legs Balsamo jumps up to hijack them), and later, once Roland and Corinne have fled Joseph Balsamo and Mary, there is an intertitle (shot 62) of 9572.6 Km. The next shot, 63, shows the car, with the camera on the hood as in shot 55, and the top still down, while Corinne tells

Roland "See? The sun's shining" (see figs. 5.11, 5.12, and 5.13). The titles suggest they have traveled 45 kilometers, but whether it was in the sun or rain, and with or without Joseph and Mary is all left unresolved.

If this were a normal, linear cause-and-effect diegesis the time of narrating would be more unified. There should be some indication that the entire Balsamo scene was a memory or fantasy, but instead it stands as a fantastic insert. There is not another time-reading intertitle until Sunday, after Roland and Corinne have already been travelling on foot. So the similarity of scenes 6 and 8, and the conversation in each, indicate that the Balsamo incident never occurred, or at least not at five or six o'clock that Saturday afternoon. According to diegetic indices such as the characters' dialogue and the condition of the car, Balsamo's scene does not seem to come at the "right place" in the story, but no cues announce when it should occur.

The editing strategy here signals overtly that there are inconsistencies in the ordering of events, and therefore, the fictional time is complicated by the editing. The time of the scenes cannot be reconstructed except by privileging the order of the shots as correct and by depending on already untrustworthy intertitles to designate time and space. The inconsistencies cannot be resolved here any easier than in Godard's example of the navy admiral wearing Davy Crocket's hat: we are left asking whether Balsamo was really present on that Saturday afternoon.

The editing pattern itself is even more disruptive in its presentation of Roland and Corinne's car crash. This scene (8), resembles the fragmented arrival of the police in *Alphaville*, and proceeds as follows:

Shot 67: tracking shot ahead of Roland and Corinne's car as they chase a white car off the road, and are about to hit a chicken.

Honking continues throughout the scene on the soundtrack.

Shot 68: a seven-frame medium-long shot of three cars burning (see fig. 5.14). (Roland is visible upside down in the left car's driver's seat.)

Shot 69: same as 67, but now chicken is being flung across the road in front of car (see fig. 5.15).

Sound of racing car engines joins with the honking.

Shot 70: same burning cars as 68, again seven frames long.

165

Fig. 5.11. Roland: "Don't annoy me. I said it's going to rain."

Fig. 5.12. Roland picks up Mary Madeleine

Fig. 5.13. Corinne: "See? The sun's shining."

Shot 71: Roland and Corinne's car swerving in the same tracking shot.

Shot 72: same burning cars, now only six frames long.

Shot 73: the car moves closer to tracking camera, still swerving, eleven frames.

Corinne: "My Hermes handbag!"

Shot 74: same burning cars, but now Corinne and Roland crawl out of one car and exit to the left.

These short bursts of flash-forwards to Roland and Corinne's own car wreck, intercut with the "before the crash" details, create a different time scheme in *Weekend*. This tracking shot, like the travelling shot of the traffic jam, has ellipses of its own—we never see the chicken actually get hit. In fact, the inserts of the burning cars seem to act as cuts to a simultaneous event, since the short shot lengths of six and seven frames are roughly equivalent to the ellipses of the driving shot. Thus, while

Fig. 5.14. Burning cars (shot 68)

Fig. 5.15. Driving past tractor (shot 69)

this sequence appears to be a rigid alternating syntagma, it also recalls the travelling shot of scene 4 via its visible ellipses. It becomes impossible to make any hypothesis concerning where these burning cars are until the sequence is over. The short time gaps and apparent mismatches between car shots (the car does not appear to be any further along the road in shot 69 than in 67, even though the chicken has been moved), help to create a strange discontinuity.

A third sort of multiplication of the narrative voices is offered by the Third World sequence, in which the garbage workers recite Fanon, Carmichael, and Engels. On an immediately concrete level there is the narrative device of separating the words from the speakers: The African speaks off-screen for his silent "Arab brother" who is on-screen, and the Arab speaks for the African. This is a central scene to the overall concept of *Weekend*, because it overtly cites some of the sources from which the film is constructed, such as Engels's early writings on the Iroquois. Yet the speeches are undercut by the staging and editing patterns which illustrate, compete with, and even contradict the words being spoken.

Scene 16 opens with a political lesson wherein the two workers refuse to share their sandwiches with Roland and Corinne, except by following the patterns set up between the West and Africa—Corinne has to kiss the Arab (Laslo Szabo) first, and then get kicked before they can have any food (see fig. 5.16) The Algerian "speaks" first, through the off-screen, close-miked black worker. Thus the voice is doubly removed: it is from an off-screen character and the voice sounds like a voice-over in opposition to all other dialogue in the film. (In the American release print there is a further distancing since the voices are dubbed in English, making this the film's only scene without subtitles.) During this speech about the West's spiritual and physical liquidation of the African people, there are shots inserted from earlier in the film: Balsamo chases Roland's car away, St. Just speaks in the field, and Roland and Corinne walk past burning cars.

During the African's much longer speech about the necessity for guerrilla warfare, the contradiction of capitalism, and the theories of progress in Engels and Morgan, there are more shots from earlier in the film: burning cars, the dead bodies that caused the traffic jam, the neighbor with his dog and shotgun, and Joseph Balsamo surrounded by sheep, among others. But there are also shots of Roland and Corinne sitting bored on the garbage truck, and sound effects such as airplane engines, as well as occasional musical interventions. All these sounds and

Fig. 5.16. Arab garbage worker

Fig. 5.17. Roland and Corinne on garbage truck

images distract from, or complicate, the African's monologue (see fig. 5.17).

Hence the scene rapidly becomes quite complex, and the multiple levels of signification—dialogue, flashbacks, intertitles, music—all work to muddle and mock rather than illustrate any specific political message. Godard has written that *Weekend* presents a complex situation: "Showing a mixture clearly is a fairly difficult task, yet that is the sort of cinema I have always tried to create."[49] The complexity in this scene leads to an inconclusive argument on the future of the Third World and the progression of civilization as a whole. The conflicting narrative voices help this scene avoid any single, coordinating or dominant point of view which could organize the various discourses. The individual speeches are indeed given great attention in terms of film time, yet the inserts and disruptions undercut their meaning: their interference is caused partly by information overload (it becomes easier to recognize and remember scenes quoted from earlier in the film than follow the spoken arguments), and partly by the inherent criticism of those arguments in the images (Roland and Corinne look bored, and the ridiculous Balsamo is shown while the African speaks about the great Greek civilizations).

By looking at three of the twenty-one shots of the Third World dialogue we can begin to understand better how the meaning of the dialogue "slides" away from its object. In shot 129, the Arab is speaking for the black, and is discussing the contradictions of capitalism and the progression from slavery to feudalism to capitalism. During this section of the speech, part of the traffic jam tracking shot is shown, including a horse cart standing in the long string of cars. Next, in shot 130, the voice-over quotes from Engels' discussion of the inequities of the wage system, but the image is of Roland, sitting stranded and bored atop the garbage truck. And in shot 131, while the voice quotes Engels, saying that, "society has passed from barbarism to civilization," the accompanying image is from scene 3, with the neighbor running out of his apartment with a hunting dog and shotgun.

These three shots illustrate, in condensed fashion, the competition for our attention during the Third World dialogue. The horse cart may act as a signifier of ancient, feudal times, yet it looks absurd in the traffic jam scene. Rather than illustrate any point of the evolution of labor from slavery to wages, it acts as an arbitrary symbol of the past and present. Cutting to an impatient Roland further distracts from the conversation since it reinforces the potential boredom of the scene; yet it also posits

Roland as a representative of the capitalist wage system. Finally, the shot of the man with the shotgun, protecting his property and wife, is a comical contradiction of the accompanying quote about society having evolved from barbarism to civilization. Together these three images offer only remote and tangential illustrations of the weighty concepts being discussed.

The intrusion of such images, some comical, some obscure, and others reflecting the internal audience of Roland and Corinne's boredom, reinforces what Scarpetta calls the "irritation" of this sequence.[50] Rather than giving a clear, well-supported presentation of Morgan and Engels's theories on social advancement, *Weekend* offers a "confused mixture." The scene stands as an example of a heterogeneous sequence since it fits Waugh's observation that a modern text is a composite of "discourses that *always* to some extent question and relativize each other's authority."[51] The variety of images and sounds remains a collection of comments and perspectives, each of which competes with the others.

In Bakhtin's own example of the dialogic he cites one novel's rendering of dialogue by a priest, a peasant, and shopkeeper, in which each expresses his own views on a common event. In this collection of personal discourses no individual is privileged as more correct than the others so they all stand as equal voices. "Every discourse has its own owner—interested and partial."[52] Similarly, the Third World scene contains Roland and Corinne's perspective, as well as the Arab and African's, and it also has a wide variety of intertitles, inserted shots and sound effects, each interrupting the scene in its own way. Out of this collection of voices there is no hierarchy to privilege one message over the others.

In the end, these examples of contradictory intertitles, elliptical editing patterns (such as the rain in the Balsamo scene), and the plurivocal Third World sequence, force the fragmentation and rejection of a single dominant narrating voice, which is replaced by a plurality of voices. Waugh calls this sort of composite style "aleatory writing," and observes that it "responds with a reply in kind to the pluralistic, hyperactive multiplicity of styles that constitute the surfaces of present-day culture."[53] By rejecting a primary narrative voice, and emphasizing the multiplicity of the text's narrative strategies, Open Text films necessitate a sort of collage construction similar to a Godard film's "bits and pieces." This composite, dynamic style in *Weekend*, allows us to approach the second large trait of the Open Text's narrative discourse, which is its lack of closure, necessitated by its "work-in-progress" construction.

Weekend's Open Text Ending

Conventional texts rely upon stereotypical and formulaic endings to reaffirm the audience's expectations about fiction and reality. But metafictions, or fictions that reflect upon narrative traditions and processes, use their endings to disturb rather than reaffirm reading and interpretation. For Waugh, "the sense of an ending" is denied in these works and the reader is reminded of the "fictional construction of any represented world."[54] Similarly, one of the most significant characteristics of the Open Text film's ending is that a framing device is not added to close the film. The "work-in-progress" and collage nature of such films as *Weekend* and *The Man Who Lies* is therefore guaranteed by the open ending.

The entire final section of *Weekend*, involving the revolutionary FLSO camp, is left fragmented and open. While the last segments of the film occasionally show Roland or Corinne, they also represent other characters and events which could not be immediately related to Roland or Corinne's whereabouts. Just before the last scene, Roland and the pig have both been slaughtered, there has been the Arizona Jules gun-battle, and Kalfon has lost his mate (see fig. 5.18). Then the final scene begins to concentrate once again on Corinne. But, as mentioned earlier, this centering on Corinne is only begun, never accomplished.

During these final scenes Corinne is involved in the gunfight, then listens to Kalfon speaking about the horror of man, finally she is told she is eating parts of Roland and the British tourists. In contrast to the narrowing focalization in *The 400 Blows*, *Weekend* only manages to find Corinne once again, show a few glimpses of her activities, and then stop. There is no unifying of the narrative strategies; instead the ironic "Fin du Cinéma" title reminds the spectator of the constructed nature of both this tale and the cinema in general.

Part of this lack of closure comes from a rejection of formulaic narrative patterns, and the simultaneous refusal to give the audience a unified spectating position. As mentioned earlier, much of this aesthetic is motivated by an attempt to circumvent traditional forms, and thus the Open Text films often satisfy the criteria set up by *Cahiers* and *Cinéthique* during the late 1960s. Those two journals praised "films struggling at the level of the form as well as at the level of content, seek[ing] to break

Fig. 5.18. Kalfon's wounded girlfriend

down traditional ways of thinking about the world, of seeing the world and representing the world."[55] The end of *Weekend*, with its abrupt conclusion of Corinne eating Roland, its "fin du conte/cinema" titles, its music track which seems oblivious to the end of the image, and the control number, creates a collection of signifiers of "the end" which do not build together into a single homogeneous "sense of an ending."

But a second reason for this inconclusive ending comes from *Weekend*'s own specific narrative strategy or cluster of strategies. Throughout this discussion I have referred to the many story elements and discursive tactics that have interrupted both the story line and the narration. These interruptions helped open up the time, space, and logic of events and undercut the actual telling of the tale. These various interventions finally operate on a textual level to create a theme of interruption and incompletion. Character development and story progression are both constantly suspended so the story parodies the classical quest or journey. Entire scenes, like Corinne's sexual fantasy monologue and Balsamo's apparition become lodged between more linear scenes, while other events, like the "Musical Action" or the Third World sequences simply delay story progression. Contradictory intertitles and elliptical editing patterns work within scenes, disrupting the flow of images while fragmenting and challenging the telling of the story. As Raymond Lefèvre observed, *Weekend* uses a whole array of techniques to slow down and interfere with its own narrative production. According to Lefèvre, the film proceeds by "breaking the linear story by its use of intertitles, ellipses, by its juxtaposition of eccentric events and images, by intertextual citations . . . and by technical provocations such as mismatches."[56] Such a lively collection of cinematic techniques for disruption (with Godard rarely using the same kinds of interruption twice), builds toward an overall structure of irresolution and openness.

Weekend's ending continues rather than concludes this production of an Open Text by stopping our scene on Corinne eating Roland, then adding several intertitles announcing the end and presenting the control number. There is nothing in the rhythm of the final scene, in its music or in its endtitles, that creates a termination effect. *Weekend* does not even use a list of end credits to close off its narrative discourse. The story and its telling are suspended, the music drones on without crescendo, and the certificate of control is displayed in the same manner as all the other intertitles of the film.

The film ends, therefore, as it existed; it is a collection of filmic elements that are not finally intertwined into a conclusive framing device. There are indeed pieces of a story, but *Weekend*'s narrative discourse does not promise the spectator that the pieces fit together, nor does it even suggest that these are all the right pieces. The result of this abrupt, anti-epilogue ending in *Weekend* is that the spectator is not given a privileged, final spectating position that can allow a termination of the film's narrative strategies.

The stylistic diversity of *Weekend* resembles the tendency in other Godard films to keep a film open and evolving from beginning to end, thus avoiding a formulaic ending. The ending of *Weekend* may, therefore, be seen as the dismantling of a cinematic ending into potential closure devices while at the same time it is the culmination of a text about incompleteness. In typically Godardian logic, this inconclusive ending becomes an "other end," fitting the unconventional logic of Open Text films.

In *Plaisir du texte*, Barthes defines modernism as two-sided, and writes that the subversive violent side *deflates* the other side which is coded as "culture,"[57] yet culture always resists destruction by its persistent appearance within the signifiers of even the most modern of texts. The pleasure arrives in the form of this failure or break between the two sides of modernity, and their "fading" into one another. Similarly,

175

Weekend, with its opening of the text by excessive intertextual references, and its difficult scenes and unconventional narrative strategies, struggles to confront and undercut cultural and cinematic norms at every step. For Godard, the cinema must break conventional codes while confronting cultural standards as well, so the use of dispersed, open endings in his films fits his statement that, "You have to return to zero, but see that the zero has moved, that it isn't a zero anymore."[58] Such notions of a sort of fictional relativity demand that Godard's films stay productive, dialogic, and open in both their narration and their endings. *Weekend* becomes a perfect example of a truly Open Text film as it fights against conventions of closure, but also fiction and culture on the levels of both the signified and the signifier.

CHAPTER 6

CONCLUSIONS

"Do you believe that every story must have a beginning and
an end?" In ancient times a story could end only in two ways:
having passed all tests, the hero and heroine married, or else
they died. The ultimate meaning to which all stories refer has
two faces: the continuity of life, the inevitability of death.
—Italo Calvino[1]

During the late 1970s, an entire issue of *Nineteenth-Century Fiction* was
dedicated to "Closure in the Novel." That special issue was inspired by
Frank Kermode's *The Sense of an Ending*, and the renewed critical
interest in narrative closure Kermode's work inspired. In the foreword,
Alexander Welsh praised the wealth of articles and books that had
indeed been generated on the subject of endings during the decade since
Kermode's book, yet he was forced to admit that there still remained
an uncomfortable inefficiency and inconsistency within the critical vocabulary on endings.[2] Those gaps have not been closed in narrative
theory since the late 1970s either.

The fact that there was still disagreement within literary studies
itself over ways to describe and analyze novelistic and poetic endings
made the adoption of literary terms into critical film vocabulary even
more difficult than usual. This book, however, forges vocabulary and
methodology for understanding the textual and spectating activities that
produce or threaten narrative closure. In addition to setting down a
rigorous system of analysis for narrative film endings, I have also proposed a modified semiotic approach to film narratology.

The distinction between story resolution and discursive closure
helps us group narrative texts by their overall strategies of openness or

conclusiveness. My four categories—Closed Text, Open Story, Open Discourse and Open Text—allow for a primary critical operation, which is the identification of patterns of narrative resolution / irresolution and discursive openness or closure. If we apply this model consistently we can understand more fully any given film's overall narrative strategy in relation to other films with similar structures, techniques, and patterns. Thus the process of film analysis always involves the active identification of large transtextual traits and then finally the identification and study of a specific film's particular structure or network of story components and discursive techniques. These categories are not meant to rule out all borderline cases, however, since many films struggle against an easily perceived definition of the degree of closure or resolution, and each viewer finally may interpret various narrative elements differently.

Instances of films that seem to slide between two categories will, and should, result from a study like this. One illustrative example would be Mike Nichols's *The Graduate* (1967), whose rather playfully loose story construction seems strongly influenced by the French New Wave. In the final scene, Ben Braddock (Dustin Hoffman) has won Elaine Robinson (Katherine Ross) away from Carl Smith, the man she just married, and her family. In a moment of euphoria Ben and Elaine escape on a city bus and ride away together. The story certainly has resolved the major hermeneutic of Ben's goal. However, during the final shots of their ride on the bus the characters never really pay attention to one another (when Ben looks to Elaine she is looking away seriously, when Elaine looks at Ben he is smiling off in a different direction). Moreover, instead of a happy reprise, the soundtrack plays "The Sounds of Silence" which has been reserved for sad or lonely moments when Ben was confused. Thus, though the film is firmly closed on the discursive level, the happy ending is undercut by their performance, the soundtrack, and the fact that they have no where to go.

The Graduate's story is at once complete and incomplete. The degree of resolution is a function of which story parameters the viewer privileges. Virginia Wright Wexman argues that the promise of a romantic union at the end of a film is often so powerful that it can provide the audience a "satisfying sense of closure" despite gaps and confusion in the story. However, if we stick to my methodology and trace back themes from across the film, we can argue that *The Graduate* does belong in the Open Story category, partly because of the sombre tone: Ben has finally decided what he wants in the second half of the film—Elaine— but he does not seem satisfied with achieving that goal. It is also less than resolved since many questions remain: in addition to wondering where they, like Antoine Doinel, will go from here, we have to wonder if "the make-out king" Smith's fraternity buddies were at all correct in assuming Elaine may be pregnant. *The Graduate* thereby provides an interesting test case of a film that actively challenges the classical plot's order and ability to provide any certainty at the end while it simultaneously seems to offer story resolution. But as I have argued, the spectator as analyst finally decides how resolved or open a film is.

The Closed Text category, which included *The Quiet Man* as a specific object of study, was presented as the dominant and most conventional group of films, but that category should not be assumed to be either static or easily summarized. My analysis of the so-called classical cinema is certainly centered around its traits of resolution and closure, yet should never be considered as a monolithic group style or strategy. Throughout this book I have treated the Closed Text as a sort of stable building block for helping construct an understanding of the production and interpretation of the other three categories, but future work with film endings should examine in far more detail the widely diverse film styles and generic and historical parameters of Closed Text films.

The other three categories have necessarily appeared more dynamic since they are attempts at dividing more modernist "art" films into more specific groups for analysis. In *Reading for the Plot*, Peter Brooks points out that the more recent and demanding text "understands endings to be artificial, arbitrary . . . casual and textual rather than cosmic and definitive;"[3] hence we learn more about narrative and the multiple functions of endings by devoting three fourths of this study to films that challenge most actively conventional resolution and closure. As I mentioned in the introduction, one of the reasons for this study was to move away from the unproductive sliding scale of "open" and "closed" films. By positing four categories, all the non-classical films are tested in more detail for their systems of resolution and closure in order to distinguish one film's signifying practices and inscribed viewing processes from those of another. Thus the division of films into Open Story, and Open Text categories accomplishes an important initial task by separating films according to very basic narrative similarities and differences. Modern texts have invented new forms for avoiding or bypassing the necessity for closure, according to Armine Kotin Mortimer, and that is one of the motivating factors for my latter three categories.[4]

The Open Discourse category remains an area of theoretical hypothesis and conjecture. While none of the films I discussed in that chapter can individually fulfill all the characteristics of the Open Discourse film, when taken together they collectively offer a rather schematic outline of the narrative traits required of a film with a resolved story and open narrative discourse. Moreover, while all four categories are designed as ways to begin analyzing the narrative cinema for patterns of closure and resolution, the Open Discourse category allows us to consider a narrative relationship between story and narrative discourse that is not commonly used, and which, given the interpretative nature of film viewing, may be nearly impossible to locate and define.

My study has also posited a very active spectator, one who perceives and interprets the film as it unfolds, and who also applies hypotheses based upon past spectating and lived experiences. The viewer, like the film critic, works by perception, interpretation, hypothesis-making and retrospection to make sense of, and interact with, any given film text. Resolution and closure then become functions of the spectator, and, depending on background and past narrative experience, some of us will impose resolution where others will grant open ambiguity. The spectator may try, and even succeed, at interpreting the ends of open story line films, like *The 400 Blows* and *Weekend*, as relatively resolved, by retrospectively reading the final actions as metaphorical completions of the films' themes and stories. Hence for some, the textual markers may suggest that these stories are incomplete and suspended, while other spectators, especially those inspired to find unity in all things, may interpret these endings as complete, symbolic, and conclusive. As Edward Branigan points out, spectators routinely struggle to tie together even random events: "No matter how disparate the image and sound (are there even common units?), their mere juxtaposition within the boundary of a film—a syntagmatic relation created by brute force— means the reader will try to discover a relation. . . . Thus a syntagmatic relation always has some consequences for meaning."[5]

The mere order of sounds and images forces the audience to relate constantly what is being seen or heard to what has recently been perceived as well as to what is about to follow and drives comprehension forward. Peter Brooks eloquently summarizes the audience's role in organizing textual meaning: "If the motor of narrative is desire, totalizing, building ever-larger units of meaning, the ultimate determinants of meaning lie *at the end*, and narrative desire is ultimately, inexorably, desire *for* the end."[6] When a film ends suddenly, or without resolving major plot lines or giving cues of closure, viewers may nonetheless continue their production process of weaving various story events together in order to finish off their interpretation of the narrative. Instead of accepting a static spectator who is completely "positioned and inscribed" by the film process, as many semioticians handily define their subject, we must account for what Francesco Casetti describes as "a conscious partner who recognizes the task s/he is given," eventually achieving a competence at interpreting a text as a sort of mutual game.[7]

The study of narrative texts has altered the conception of the reader-viewer throughout its evolution, redefining the spectator from being an organic individual to an invisible and metaphorical position or place to an unconscious processor of the collective, cultural imaginary. The dramatic inroads made by cognitive psychology and reception theory within film studies offer strong evidence that structuralist, psychoanalytic, and semiotic conceptions of the spectator have proven incomplete. The shift in film studies is away from theorizing the audience as a monolithic body of subjects all sharing the same drives, fears, and cultural determinations.

One realm of narrative analysis that this book has not considered to the extent that it deserves attention is the area of the ideological implications of endings. However, this entire study has been implicitly influenced by Jean-Pierre Oudart's article "L'Ideologie moderniste dans quelques films recents." Oudart outlines the classical Hollywood cinema's use of secure resolution and closure to help reaffirm dominant ideology by ensuring an ending that reestablishes social order.[8] The central ideological conflicts between economics and ideology in Oudart's criticism of the Hollywood cinema are often seen as displaced onto sexual thematic oppositions: The threatening option or force must be repressed so an imaginary resolution can reunite the community of the film and thus American society as a whole. Oudart interprets the duel to the death in a western like *My Darling Clementine* as a prime metaphor for the classical cinema's need of a fixed discursive figure that can triumphantly terminate the battle between deviant forces competing over the future of their community. Thus the ritual killing of the western's "bad guy," like the romantic comedy's reuniting of lovers, or science fiction's death of the "mad doctor," reaffirms dominant ideology and covers over the contradictions of society.[9]

In a broader sense, the very investigation of endings puts into question the concepts of realism or plausibility in the rendering of social patterns of narrativity, and any such analysis is, as Alexander Welsh writes, "haunted by the possibility that the language and logic in which those problems are posed dictate conclusiveness where none may really

181

exist."[10] Thus, the issues raised by the study of endings involve how closure and resolution are determined by both film practice or language, and ideological factors.

I do not pretend that this book has in any way exhausted the notions of closure in the cinema. It has, however, accomplished what it set out to do, which was to distinguish four theoretical categories in order to understand better the strategies of story resolution and discursive closure. Simultaneously, my work here is an effort to combat the inconsistency in narratology's vocabulary and methodology for the analysis of endings. The interest in endings, therefore, should continue to expand in relation to how a spectator processes textual sounds and images as they are perceived and related to other sounds and images. The final operation of a film viewer is always to interpret the end of a film against the immediate text's story and narrative discourse, as well as the narrative strategies of past and future textual and extratextual experience. In the end, notions of closure in the cinema challenge conceptions of text, story, narration, and viewing in order to continue rather than conclude our interest in endings.

Finally, Roland Barthes's observation regarding his own fascination with endings may be the most fitting tactic for concluding my study of how films end: "I take pleasure in hearing myself tell a story *whose ending I already know*: I know and yet I do not know. I pretend, for myself, as if I did not know: I know very well that Oedipus will be unmasked, that Danton will be guillotined, *but at the same time . . .*"[11]

Segmentation for *The Quiet Man*

Director: John Ford; **Producers:** Herbert J. Yates, John Ford & Merian C. Cooper's Argosy Productions; **Screenplay:** Frank S. Nugent; **Photography:** Winton C. Hoch; **Music:** Victor Young; Technicolor (1952).

1. (shot 1) Opening titles over picture of a boat in a bay.

Fade

2. (shots 2–23) Train station. Sean Thornton arrives and asks the local people how to get to Innisfree. Michaleen Og Flynn appears mysteriously and takes Sean's bags to his waiting cart. Father Lonergan begins narrating in voice-over and the locals watch Sean leave, wondering aloud why anyone would want to go to Innisfree.

Dissolve

3. (shots 24–37) On the road. Sean is driven from the train by Michaleen Flynn. On the trip Sean sees his home and vows to buy it back, beginning to answer the question of why he has come to Ireland.

Dissolve

4. (shots 38–70) On the road. Father Lonergan resumes his narrating as he approaches the cart, is introduced to Sean, and promises to remember Sean's mother in tomorrow's mass. Sean and Mary Kate exchange glances as she leads sheep home. In town Sean is taken into Cohan's Pub.

Fade

5. (shots 71–86) Sunday morning at the church. Sean learns Mary Kate's name and finds out about her lack of a fortune. Sean offers her a hand full of holy water, as church and religion become aids to their romance. Michaleen scolds him and mentions the formal courting rituals followed in Ireland.

Dissolve

6. (shots 87–111) The Widow Sarah Tillane's house. Sean asks to buy White O'Morn and tells her "Innisfree has come to mean heaven to me." Then Will Danaher arrives and tries to outbid him. Will angers Sarah Tillane by mentioning their mutual romantic interests, so she lets Sean buy the cottage and land.

7. (shots 112–25) The Danaher house. Mary Kate is serving the workers' meals when Will vows revenge on Sean for buying the neighboring land. Mary Kate defends Sean's right to the land.

8. (shots 126–67) Cohan's Bar. Sean offers everyone in Cohan's a drink, mentioning his lineage. Will enters and challenges Sean to fight and warns him to stay away from Mary Kate. Sean refuses and Father Lonergan arrives to re-route it to a handshake. Everyone sings "Jack Duggin" in Sean's honor.

9. (shots 168–94) Evening. Michaleen and Sean walk toward White O'Morn. Sean enters and finds Mary Kate has cleaned the house and is hiding there. They embrace, then she runs home.

Fade

10. (shots 195–222) White O'Morn, morning. Sean has repaired his home and the bed is delivered. The Rev. Playfair and his wife approve of his efforts and Mary Kate watches the bed's arrival from over a fence.

11. (shots 223–56) The Danaher house. Michaleen Flynn comes as matchmaker to Mary Kate's house, and Mary Kate gives permission for Sean to come courting.

Dissolve

12. (shots 257–79) The Danaher house, evening. Michaleen and Sean call on Will and Mary Kate, but he refuses to allow Sean to court Mary Kate, thus denying her dowry. The two men leave in the rain.

Fade

13. (shots 280–94) Countryside. Lonergan, in voice-over, tells of Sean riding angrily on horseback and that some of the men decided to plot against Will Danaher.

14. (shots 295–371) Innisfree Race. Sean wins and takes the Widow's hat instead of Mary Kate's, making the jealous Will decide that it is better for Sean to marry Mary Kate than Will's own object of desire. The Rev. Playfair realizes that Sean is the fighter Trooper Thorn.

Dissolve

15. (shots 372–419) Innisfree streets. Will allows Sean and Mary Kate to court, so they ride in Michaleen's wagon, but escape on a tandem bicycle.

16. (shots 420–42) On the road. Sean and Mary Kate ride the bicycle, run across the Kabrook, and embrace in the storm.

Fade

17. (shots 443–92) The Wedding at the Danaher house. Will finds out he was tricked and that the Widow has not promised to marry him, so he refuses to give the bride's dowry to Mary Kate. Sean denounces the dowry but is knocked out by Will. There is a flashback to Sean in the ring as we learn he was a boxer and killed a man in the ring (this sequence consists of 15 shots in 92 seconds). Rev. Playfair helps Sean up, Sean and Mary Kate leave solemnly.

Dissolve

18. (shots 493–504) The cottage, their wedding night. Mary Kate refuses to let Sean touch her until she has her dowry, she locks herself in the bedroom. He kicks in the door and throws her on the bed, but then leaves the room.

Fade

19. (shots 505–18) The cottage, next morning. Sean has slept in his sleeping bag, but when Michaleen and friends bring the furniture she asks him to hide the bag. They have not brought the money. Sean disappoints Mary Kate by saying he doesn't care about the money. Michaleen sees the broken bed, misinterprets the cause and mutters, "Homeric!"

184

Dissolve

20. (shots 519–27) White O'Morn. Sean is going to plant roses but Mary Kate wants vegetables, while Sean wants children more than the roses. They cheer up and decide to walk to Castletown to shop.

Dissolve

21. (shots 528–41) White O'Morn. Sean honks for Mary Kate from the new horse and buggy he has bought her as a wedding gift. They drive to town, but when Sean refuses to beg Will for the money Mary Kate calls him a coward and rides off alone in the buggy. Sean has to walk home.

22. (shots 542–56) Castletown. Mary Kate and Sean head home separately in alternation. Mary Kate finds Father Lonergan fishing and explains her problem in Irish. He scolds her for making Sean sleep in a bag instead of a bed and loses a fish in anger.

Dissolve

23. (shots 557–78) Sean walks to Cohan's Bar, but then refuses to fight Will for the second time in public.

24. (shots 579–95) Rev. Playfair's house. Sean visits Rev. Playfair and is encouraged to fight for his wife's love. Trooper's past is fully explained and his motives or options about fighting are discussed.

Dissolve

25. (shots 596–98) White O'Morn. Sean and Mary Kate sit in front of the fireplace and try to understand each other. They begin to act affectionate.

Fade

26. (shots 599–608) Morning at White O'Morn, Sean learns from Michaleen that Mary Kate has left for the train in shame.

27. (shots 609–65) The train station. Mary Kate climbs into the train which is delayed by arguing engineers. Sean arrives and pulls her off the train, so people follow them across the countryside. Sean brutally drags Mary Kate back to Will. Will still refuses to give up the money so Sean throws Mary Kate back to him explaining the deal is off. Will finally pays up but Sean throws the money in the fire.

28. (shots 666–734) The farm. Sean and Mary Kate begin to exit but Will attacks Sean who knocks Will down. The fight begins as the now proud Mary Kate heads home. The fight moves across country to Innisfree, with a large crowd (including Rev. Playfair and his Bishop) betting on the outcome. After a brief rest and drink at Cohan's, Sean realizes it is dinner time, so knocks Will through Cohan's door.

29. (shots 735–43) Rev. Playfair's house. The Rev. Playfair, his wife and the Bishop settle their bets.

Dissolve

30. (shots 744–46) The Kabrook at White O'Morn. Sean and Will stumble home to the waiting Mary Kate for dinner. Sean says, "Woman of the house I have brought the brother home for dinner." Will says "God bless all in this house."

Dissolve and Lonergan's Voice-Over

31. (shots 747–67) Epilogue—The bridge in town. Lonergan's narration moves into the present. Playfair and the Bishop pass by, then Will and Widow Tillane in the courting cart. The film's characters pose for the end, and finally Sean and Mary Kate wave, then turn and run back into the cottage.

185

APPENDIX B

Segmentation for *THE 400 BLOWS*

Director: Francois Truffaut; **Producers:** S.E.D.I.F. and Les Films du Carrosse; **Screenplay:** Francois Truffaut and Marcel Moussy; **Photography:** Henri Decae; **Music:** Jean Constantin (1959).

1. (shots 1–9) Title Sequence: titles are superimposed over the nine travelling shots of Paris and the Eiffel Tower.

2. (shots 10–51) Antoine's classroom. Antoine is caught with a pin-up picture and sent to the corner where he writes that he is being unjustly punished. After recess the teacher makes them write out a poem while Antoine cleans the wall. Finally, René and Antoine go home.

Dissolve

3. (shots 52–73) The Doinel Apartment. Antoine's mother scolds him and sends him for flour. Returning, he and Mr. Doinel enter together, all three of them have dinner. The parents argue about what she does in the afternoon, and Antoine ends the evening taking out the garbage.

Fade

4. (shots 74–118) Morning. Antoine has not finished his assignment, so he and René spend the day at the movies and the amusement park, but afterwards they see Mrs. Doinel kissing some man on the street. Mauricet, another boy in the class, spies on the boys as René gives Antoine an old excuse to copy for the teacher.

5. (shots 119–24) The apartment that evening. Mr. Doinel and Antoine fix dinner that evening since Mrs. Doinel will be home "late." Antoine is woken up when she comes home and overhears their argument in which Antoine's illegitimacy is mentioned. He hears his mother threaten to send him away to boarding school.

Fade

6. (shots 125–39) Morning at the apartment. After Antoine leaves for school, Mauricet visits the apartment, pretending to be asking after Antoine's health. The parents learn he missed school the day before.

7. (shots 140–58) At school. Antoine tells the teacher that he was absent because his mother died, but once class begins, Mr. and Mrs. Doinel arrive. Mr. Doinel slaps Antoine.

187

Dissolve

8. (shots 159–76) Evening. The Doinels find Antoine's farewell note, he has decided to run away. René finds Antoine a print shop in which to sleep. Later, Antoine wanders the Paris streets, steals a bottle of milk, and washes up in a frozen fountain.

9. (shots 177–204) School the next day. Mrs. Doinel comes to school and pulls Antoine out of English class, taking him home. She promises to pay him if he gets a good French composition grade.

Fade

10. (shots 205–23) School the next day. The gym teacher takes the children for a run but the boys gradually evade him a la *Zéro de conduite*.

Fade

11. (shots 208–23) At school, Antoine writes his composition, during which there is the subjective voice-over as he recites the end of the Balzac novel. That evening, Antoine makes an altar for Balzac, but it starts a fire. Later that evening the family goes to *Paris Nous appartient*, and they all return happy.

Fade

12. (shots 224–37) Next day at school. The teacher accuses Antoine of copying Balzac, and sends him to the principal, but he escapes on the way. René leaves school with him.

Dissolve

13. (shots 238–80) Same evening at René's house. René hides Antoine at his house and saves food for him. The boys steal money to go see a puppet show and movie.

Fade

14. (shots 281–345) Antoine and René steal the typewriter, but cannot sell it so they return it. Antoine is caught. Mr. Doinel takes Antoine to the local police station where Antoine spends the night until taken to the central police station.

15. (shots 346–55) Mrs. Doinel meets with a judge. She explains that Antoine is not her husband's son. The judge and mother agree that several months of observation in a detention home is in order.

Fade

16. (shots 356–68) Antoine is at the Centre d'Observation de Mineurs Delinquents. He is slapped for eating before he is told, and later listens to the reasons the other boys are there. An escapee is returned.

Fade

17. (shots 369–75) Antoine visits the psychiatrist. In a series of lap-dissolves, Antoine talks about his past and admits that his mother wanted an abortion.

18. (shots 376–96) René and Mrs. Doinel visit the Centre. René is turned away, but Mrs. Doinel enters and tells Antoine how much his letter accusing her of being unfaithful has hurt Mr. Doinel. She also mentions that Mr. Doinel no longer wants to see Antoine and that he will be apprenticed out when he gets out of the Centre.

Dissolve

19. (shot 397–404) Soccer Game. Antoine excapes during a soccer game and runs to the sea. The film ends with an optical zoom into a freeze-frame of shot 404.

Fade

Segmentation for *Weekend*

Director: Jean-Luc Godard; **Producers:** Comacico, Les Films Copernic, Lira Films, Ascot Cineraid; **Screenplay:** Jean-Luc Godard; **Photography:** Raoul Coutard; **Music:** Antoine Duhamel, Mozart's piano sonata K 576; Eastman Color (1967).

1. (shots 1–10) Roland and Corinne's apartment. Exposition of the parallel plots to get the money from Corinne's dying father. Significant titles: "A Film lost in the cosmos," "A Film found on the scrapheap."

Fade

2. (shots 11–13) Corinne, shot in silhouette, tells her erotic tale to an undentified man. "Anal/yse."

Fade

3. (shots 14–17) "Saturday 10 AM Scene from Paris Life." Corinne and Roland bump into the neighbors' car, spray paint the woman's dress and are chased away by the man with the shotgun.

Fade

4. (shots 18–25) "Saturday 11 AM–2:10 PM." A long tracking shot of a traffic jam, intercut with temporal markings and involving some overlap between shots.

Fade

5. (shots 26–46) Roland and Corinne witness the crash of a tractor and sports car. The debate between the bourgeoise and the Communist farmer is intercut with shots of local people watching. "Fauxtographe."

6. (shots 47–55) "Saturday 3–4 PM." Roland and Corinne, driving, are again interrupted by some event, arms try to reach into their car to stop them. Corinne asks whether it will rain, and Roland replies, "yes." "95280 KM."

7. (shots 56–61) "Saturday 5 PM." Their car stops in the rain to pick up Mary Madeleine, but they are hijacked by Joseph Balsamo. He performs several miracles and Roland and Corinne finally leave him in the field of sheep.

8. (shots 62–74) "95720 KM." Continued driving shots as in segment 6, but Corinne says, "See? The sun *is* shining." Roland chases a car and bike off the road. There are short flashes forward to a car wreck. Corinne and Roland crawl out of their own crashed car.

189

9. (shots 75–76) "From the French Revolution to UNR Weekends." Roland and Corinne pass St. Just in a field reading his writings aloud. Speaking to the camera he declares, "All I see are constitutions backed by gold, pride and blood."

Fade

10. (shots 77–84) "Sunday/Monday's Story." Corinne and Roland meet and fight with Léaud, who is singing in the phone booth.

Fade

11. (shot 85) A crane shot studies Roland and Corinne walking along the road, asking dead bodies the directions to Oinville. The camera returns to the first burning car of the shot after Roland and Corinne have walked on.

Fade

12. (shots 86–103) While wandering on a country road, Roland and Corinne meet Emily Bronte and Gros Pouce. Emily questions the sciences while Tom Thumb reads poems written on scraps of paper. Finally, Roland gets frustrated and lights Emily on fire.

Fade

13. (shots 104–8) "A Tuesday in the Hundred Year's War." Roland discusses ignorance, looks at a worm, and then he and Corinne rob bodies of their designer clothes. Eventually they hitch a ride in an INNO truck.

14. (shot 109) "Action Musicale." A 360° pan around a farmyard while the truck driver plays Mozart on a piano.

15. (shots 110–17) "Week of 4 Thursdays" "A Friday far from Robinson." Corinne and Roland try hitchhiking but fail to answer the drivers' political questions correctly. Corrine is raped in a ditch by a passing bum. They eventually wander past the Italian co-workers and then are picked up by a garbage truck.

16. (shots 118–46) African history lessons. Roland and Corinne help with the garbage work, then listen as the black and Algerian workers speak for each other. Their monologues are interrupted by shots from earlier and later within the film. Roland and Corinne see a sign for Oinville.

Fade

17. (shots 147–62) Corinne takes a bath while Roland tells the tale of a hippopotamus who wants to hide in the water. Various exterior shots of Oinville are inserted. "Scenes from provincial life."

18. (shots 163–66) The mother returns from the market but refuses to split her 50 million with them, so Roland and Corinne kill her. Her blood washes over the skinned rabbit.

Fade

19. (shots 167–70) Exterior shots: the yellow Citroen passes by; there is a cut to a pile of wrecked cars and an airplane. Roland and Corinne light the pile on fire to hide the dead mother's body.

Fade

20. (shots 171–73) "Liberation Front of Seine & Oise" [FLSO]. Roland and Corinne are captured by the FLSO, along with some tourists. We meet Kalfon playing drums and Ernest the cook.

Fade

21. (shots 174–84) A woman chains some people to a tree, and a young woman, being prepared for her death, is raped with a fish. "Totem and Taboo."

22. (shots 185–200) "Light of August." Roland is killed by the gang. "September massacre," a pig is slaughtered. "October massacre," a goose is killed. Kalfon calls other groups on the radio. "Langage d'octobre."

23. (shots 201–2) A long track/pan/crane shot with Kalfon reciting Lautréamont's ode to the ocean.

190

Fade

    24. (shots 203–14) "Arizona Jules." A prisoner exchange turns into a gunfight. Kalfon's woman is killed and sings a farewell song.

Fade

    25. (shots 215–19) Kalfon explains the horror of humanity to Corinne, who then eats a concoction of tourists, pork and bits of Roland. "Fin du conte/Fin du cinéma."

NOTES

Chapter 1

1. Christian Metz, *Film Language: A Semiotics of the Cinema* (New York: Oxford Univ. Press, 1978), 17.

2. For a sample of studies on the significance of openings see Thierry Kuntzel, "Le Travail du film," *Communications* 19 (1972) and "Le Travail du film, 2," *Communications* 23 (1975), 136–89; Michel Marie, *Muriel: Histoire d'une récherche* (Paris: Galilée, 1974); Marc Vernet, "The Filmic Transaction: On the Openings of Film Noirs," *The Velvet Light Trap* 20 (Summer 1983), 2–9; and *Aesthetics of Film* (Austin: Univ. of Texas Press, 1992), 97–105; and David Bordwell and Kristin Thompson, *Film Art* (New York: McGraw-Hill, 1993), 45 and 55.

3. Barbara Herrnstein Smith, *Poetic Closure: A Study of How Poems End* (Chicago: Univ. of Chicago Press, 1968), 2.

4. Ibid., 34.

5. David H. Richter, *Fable's End: Completeness and Closure in Rhetorical Fiction*, (Chicago: Univ. of Chicago Press, 1974), 170.

6. Ibid., 178.

7. Julia Kristeva, *Le Texte du roman* (The Hague: Mouton, 1970), 50–51.

8. Umberto Eco, *L'Oeuvre ouverte* (Paris: Editions du Seuil, 1965), 306.

9. Ibid., 306.

10. Jacques Aumont, Alain Bergala, Michel Marie, and Marc Vernet, *Aesthetics of Film*, trans. Richard Neupert (Austin: Univ. of Texas Press, 1992), 84.

11. Ferdinand de Saussure, *Cours de linguistique générale* (Paris: Payot, 1979), 33.

12. Roland Barthes, "Presentation," *Communications* 4 (1964), 1.

13. For discussions and definitions of these terms see *Aesthetics of Film*, 82–85 and 95–96; Emile Benveniste, *Problèmes de linguistique gènérale* (Paris: Gallimard, 1966), 239–42; Christian Metz, *Film Language*, 25.

14. Metz, *Film Language*, 28.

15. Jonathan Culler, *The Pursuit of Signs: Semiotics, Literature, Deconstruction* (Ithaca: Cornell Univ. Press, 1981), 171.

16. Tzvetan Todorov, "Les Catégories du récit littéraire," *Communications* 8 (1966), 127.

17. Seymour Chatman, *Story and Discourse: Narrative Structure in Fiction and Film* (Ithaca: Cornell Univ. Press, 1978), 31.

18. Ibid., 43–44.

19. Ibid., 96.

20. Roland Barthes, *Image/Music/Text* (New York: Hill and Wang, 1977), 93–94.

21. Tzvetan Todorov, *The Poetics of Prose* (Ithaca: Cornell Univ. Press, 1977), 111.

22. Rick Altman, *The American Film Musical* (Bloomington: Indiana Univ. Press, 1987), 51.

23. Gerald Prince, *Narratology: The Form and Functioning of Narrative* (New York: Mouton, 1982), 157.

24. David Bordwell, *Narration in the Fiction Film* (Madison: Univ. of Wisconsin Press, 1985), 45.

25. Virginia Wright Wexman, *Creating the Couple: Love, Marriage, and Hollywood Performance* (Princeton: Princeton Univ. Press, 1992), 81.

26. Gérard Genette, *Narrative Discourse: An Essay in Method* (Ithaca: Cornell Univ. Press, 1980), 162.

27. Ibid., 30.

28. Mary Ann Doane, "The Dialogical Text: Filmic Irony and the Spectator," diss., University of Iowa, 1979, 134.

29. Barthes, *Image/Music/Text*, 83.

30. David Bordwell, "Happily Ever After, Part Two," *The Velvet Light Trap* 19 (1982), 6.

31. David Bordwell, Janet Staiger, and Kristin Thompson, *The Classical Hollywood Cinema: Film Style and Mode of Production to 1960* (New York: Columbia Univ. Press, 1985), 34.

32. Gérard Genette, *Nouveau discours du récit* (Paris: Editions du Seuil, 1983), 68.

33. André Gaudreault, "Récit scriptural, récit théatrale, récit filmique: Prolegomènes à une théorie narratologique du cinéma," diss., Paris: DERCAV Thèse de Doctorat de 3ᵉ Cycle, 1983, 214.

34. Bordwell, *Narration*, 62.

35. Edward Branigan, *Point of View in the Cinema: A Theory of Narration and Subjectivity in Classical Film* (New York: Mouton Publishers, 1984), 2.

36. Prince, *Narratology*, 178.

37. Ibid., 186.

38. Genette, *Narrative Discourse*, 228.

39. Ibid., 243.

40. Tzvetan Todorov, *Mikhail Bakhtine le principe dialogique* (Paris: Editions du Seuil, 1981), 81–82.

41. David Bordwell, "Art Cinema as a Mode of Film Practice" *Film Criticism* 4,1 (Fall 1979), 57; see also *Narration in the Fiction Film*, 29–47, and *Classical Hollywood Cinema*, 38–39.

42. Francesco Casetti, "Looking for the Spectator," *Iris* 1,2 (1983), 24–25.

43. Smith, *Poetic Closure*, 26–27.

44. Horst Ruthrof, *The Reader's Construction of Narrative* (London: Routledge and Kegan Paul, 1981), 25.

45. Ibid., 2.

46. Smith, *Poetic Closure*, 120.

47. Frank Kermode, *The Sense of an Ending* (New York: Oxford Univ. Press, 1967), 150.

48. Armine Kotin Mortimer *La Clôture narrative* (Paris: José Corti, 1985), 10.

Chapter 2

1. Yvonne Baby, "I Wanted to Treat *Shoot the Piano Player* like a Tale by Perrault: An Interview with François Truffaut," *Shoot the Piano Player* ed. Peter Brunette (New Brunswick: Rutgers Univ. Press, 1993), 129.

2. Elizabeth J. MacArthur, *Extravagant Narratives: Closure and Dynamics in the Epistolary Form* (Princeton: Princeton Univ. Press, 1990), 16.

3. Mortimer, 15.

4. Peter Brooks, *Reading for the Plot: Design and Intention in Narrative* (Cambridge: Harvard Univ. Press, 1992), 23.

5. Jacques Aumont, Alain Bergala, Michel Marie, Marc Vernet, 70.

6. Ann Jefferson, *The Nouveau Roman and the Poetics of Fiction* (New York: Cambridge Univ. Press, 1980), 61.

7. David Bordwell, Janet Staiger and Kristin Thompson, 17.

8. Chatman, 46.

9. Bordwell, *The Classical Hollywood Cinema*, 16.

10. Thierry Kuntzel, "Le Travail du film," *Communications* 23 (1975), 153.

11. See Virginia Wright Wexman, *Creating the Couple*, 81–83 and 112.

12. See Will Wright, *Sixguns and Society* (Berkeley: Univ. of California Press, 1975), 151.

13. Christian Metz, *Film Language*, 329.

14. Mary Ann Doane, "Desire in *Sunrise*" *Film Reader* 2 (January 1977), 71.

15. Thomas Schatz, *Hollywood Genres* (New York: Random House, 1981), 30.

16. Raymond Bellour, "Segmenting/Analysing," *Genre: The Musical*, ed. Rick Altman (Boston: Routledge and Kegan Paul, 1981), 103.

17. Wexman, 217–18.

18. Maureen Turim, *Flashbacks in Film: Memory and History* (New York: Routledge, 1989), 146.

19. Steve Neale, "New Hollywood Cinema," *Screen* 17,2 (Summer 1976), 121.

20. Martin Sutton, "Patterns of Meaning in the Musical," *Genre: The Musical*, Rick Altman, ed. (Boston: Routledge and Kegan Paul, 1981), 194.

21. Jacques Aumont, "Griffith, le cadre, la figure," in *Le Cinéma Américain* Raymond Bellour, ed. (Paris: Flammarion, 1980), 53.

22. Wexman, 81.

23. Claudia Gorbman, *Unheard Melodies: Narrative Film Music* (Bloomington: Indiana Univ. Press, 1987), 82.

24. Gérard Genette, *Narrative Discourse*, 186.

25. André Gaudreault, "Récit scriptural," 174.

26. Roland Barthes, *S/Z* (Paris: Editions du Seuil, 1970), 10.

27. Ibid., 162.

28. Wexman, 52.

29. André Gardies, *Le Cinéma de Alain Robbe-Grillet: Essai Semiocritique* (Paris: Editions Albatros, 1983), 79.

30. Colin MacCabe, "*Days of Hope*—A Response to Colin McArthur," *Screen* 17,1 (Spring 1976), 100.

31. Christian Metz, *The Imaginary Signifier* (Bloomington: Indiana Univ. Press, 1982), 7.

32. David Bordwell, "Happily Ever After, Part Two," 2.

33. Ibid., 7.

34. Annette Kuhn, *Women's Pictures: Feminism and Cinema* (Boston: Routledge and Kegan Paul, 1982), 34.

35. Rick Altman, "The American Film Musical: Paradigmatic Structure and Mediatory Function," in *Genre: The Musical*, ed. Rick Altman (Boston: Routledge and Kegan Paul, 1981), 197.

Chapter 3

1. François Truffaut, *The 400 Blows*, ed. David Denby (New York: Grove Press, 1969), 230.

2. John Gerlach, *Toward the End* (Alabama: Univ. of Alabama Press, 1985), 93.

3. Ibid., 89–90.

4. Pauline Kael, "Film Culture," *Shoot the Piano Player*, ed. Peter Brunette (New Brunswick: Rutgers Univ. Press, 1993), 153.

5. Mortimer, 185–86.

6. André Bazin, *What is Cinema?* Vol.2 (Berkeley: Univ. of California Press, 1971), 66.

7. Kristin Thompson, *Breaking the Glass Armor* (Princeton: Princeton Univ. Press, 1988), 228.

8. Ibid., 205.

9. David Bordwell and Kristin Thompson, *Film Art* (New York: McGraw-Hill, 1993), 482.

10. Allen Thiher, "The Existential Play in Truffaut's Early Films," in *Shoot the Piano Player*, ed. Brunette, 184.

11. Anne Gillain, "The Script of Delinquency: François Truffaut's *Les 400 coups* (1959)," in *French Film: Texts and Contexts*, ed. Susan Hayward and Ginette Vincendeau (London: Routledge, 1990), 187.

12. The Doinel Series consists of *The 400 Blows* (1959), the short *Antoine et Colette* (1964), *Stolen Kisses* (1968), *Bed and Board* (1970), and *Love on the Run* (1979).

13. Gérard Genette, *Palimpsestes* (Paris: Editions du Seuil, 1982), 186.

14. Robert Allen, *Speaking of Soap Operas* (Chapel Hill: Univ. of North Carolina Press, 1985), 14.

15. Karel Reisz and Gavin Millar, "The Technique of *Shoot the Piano Player*," in *Shoot the Piano Player*, ed. Brunette, 252.

16. The screenplay in *The 400 Blows*, ed. David Denby (New York: Grove Press, 1969), differs slightly from my own shot decoupage. Denby does not count the opening nine-shot title sequence; his shot 71 corresponds to my shots 80 and 81, since he does not count the swish-pan cut which separates the two shots; and his shots 274 and 290 are each two shots in my shot breakdown.

17. Don Allen, *Francois Truffaut* (London: Secker and Warburg, 1974), 30.

18. Gillain, "The Script of Delinquency," 195.

19. Georges Sadoul, "The Importance of Subject Matter," *The 400 Blows*, ed. David Denby (New York: Grove Press, 1969), 237.

20. Brunette, *Shoot the Piano Player*, 252.

21. Don Allen, 39.

22. Sadoul, 244.

23. François Truffaut, *Les Films de ma vie* (Paris: Editions du Cerf, 1972), 288.

24. David Bordwell, "Art Cinema as a Mode of Film Practice," 60.

25. Jean-Luc Godard, "Le Photo du mois," *Cahiers du Cinéma* 92 (February 1959), 44.

26. Jean-Paul Simon, *Le Filmique et le comique: Essai sur le film comique* (Paris: Editions Albatros, 1979), 118.

27. According to the script, the girls are "apparently children of employees of the center;" Denby, 131.

28. Jacques Rivette, "Du Côté de chez Antoine," *Cahiers du Cinéma* 95 (May 1959), 38.

29. Arlene Croce, "A Review" *Film Quarterly* 13, 3 (Spring 1960), 38.

30. Gorbman, 18.

31. Ibid., 3.

32. Alain Robbe-Grillet, *Pour un nouveau roman* (Paris: Editions du Minuit, 1963), 30.

33. Bordwell and Thompson, 479.

34. Roberto Rossellini, "A Discussion of Neo-Realism," *Screen* 14, 4 (Winter 1973–1974), 71.

35. Smith, *Poetic Closure*, 109.

36. Thompson, *Breaking the Glass Armor*, 95. She also provides an excellent scene-to-scene summary on page 103 to prove the film's dominant narrative structure.

37. Noel Burch, *Theory of Film Practice* (Princeton: Princeton Univ. Press, 1981), 64.

38. Kuhn, 137.

39. Robert Allen, 138.

40. Rivette, 38.

41. Godard, "Le Photo du mois," 44.

Chapter 4

1. Aumont, Bergala, Marie, and Vernet, 6.

2. Tzvetan Todorov, *The Fantastic: A Structural Approach to a Literary Genre* (Ithaca: Cornell Univ. Press, 1975), 13–14.

3. Ibid., 21.

4. Paul Ricoeur, *La Configuration dans le récit de fiction* (Paris: Editions du Seuil, 1984), 38.

5. James Monaco, *The New Wave* (New York: Oxford Univ. Press, 1976), 264.

6. Gavin Millar, "Claude Chabrol," *Cinema: A Critical Dictionary*, ed. Richard Roud, 2 vols. (London: Martin Secker & Warburg, 1980), 1, 196.

7. Robin Wood and Michael Wallace, *Claude Chabrol* (New York: Praeger, 1970), 56.

8. Ibid., 57.

9. Ibid., 56.

10. Joel Magny, *Claude Chabrol* (Paris: Cahiers du Cinéma, 1987), 178.

11. Monaco, 263.

12. Victor Shklovsky, "La construction de la nouvelle et du roman," *Théorie de la littérature*, ed. Tzvetan Todorov (Paris: Editions du Seuil, 1965), 176.

13. Different prints of *Earth* use different translations for the characters; I am indebted to Vance Kepley who provided the consistent Russian equivalents which I will use: Vasyl corresponds to Basil, Semyon is Simon, Piotr equals Peter, and I retain Foma Belokon rather than Thomas Whitehorse.

14. Luda and Jean Schnitzer, *Histoire du Cinéma Sovietique 1919–1940* (Paris: Pygmalion, 1979), 71.

15. Jay Leyda, *Kino* (New York: Collier Books, 1973), 275.

16. Leyda, 275.

17. Unfortunately, several 16 mm prints of *Earth* in circulation do lack the final four shots.

18. Kristin Thompson, "Sawing Through the Bough," *Wide Angle* 1,3 (1976), 49.

19. Martin Walsh, "Godard and Me: Jean-Pierre Gorin Talks," *The Brechtian Aspect of Radical Cinema* (London: BFI, 1981), 122.

20. Robert Bresson, *Notes sur le cinématographe* (Paris: Gallimard, 1975), 61.

21. David Bordwell, "Art Cinema as a Mode of Film Practice," 57.

22. Schatz, 30.

23. Ricoeur, 36.

24. Marilyn Johns Blackwell, *Persona: The Transcendent Image* (Urbana: Univ. of Illinois Press, 1986), 114.

Chapter 5

1. Robbe-Grillet, 132.

2. Barthes, *S/Z*, 10–12.

3. Kermode, *The Sense of an Ending*, 138.

4. Brooks, 315.

5. Jean-Luc Comolli and Jean Narboni, "Cinema/Ideology/Criticism," *Movies and Methods*, ed. Bill Nichols (Berkeley: Univ. of California Press, 1976), 26.

6. Mortimer, 212.

7. Hayden White, "The Value of Narrativity in the Representation of Reality," *On Narrative* ed. W. J. T. Mitchell (Chicago: Univ. of Chicago Press, 1981), 20.

8. François Vanoye, *Récit écrit-récit filmique* (Paris: Editions CEDIC, 1979), 207.

9. Ibid., 207.

10. Ibid., 208.

11. Brooks, 315.

12. Chatman, 49.

13. Patricia Waugh, *Metafiction* (London: Methuen, 1984), 10.

14. Genette, *Narrative Discourse*, 35.

15. François Jost, "Vers de nouvelles approches méthodologiques," *Cinémas de la modernité*, ed. Dominique Chateau, André Gardies, Francois Jost (Paris: Klincksieck, 1981) 32; see also Richard Neupert, "*L'Immortelle*: The Ciné-romanand the Ciné-lecteur" *French Literature Series* 17 (1990), 35–41.

16. Jost, "Vers de nouvelles approches methodologiques," 36.

17. Chatman, 57.

18. Eco, *L'Oeuvre ouverte*, 62.

19. Bordwell, *Narration in the Fiction Film*, 324.

20. Todorov, *Mikhail Bakhtine*, 8.

21. Mikhail Bakhtin, *Esthétique et théorie du roman* (Paris: Editions du Seuil, 1981), 296.

22. Iouri Lotman, *La Structure du texte artistique* (Paris: Gallimard, 1973), 309.

23. Bakhtin, "La Structure de l'énoncé" in *Mikhail Bakhtine: le principe dialogique*, ed. Tzvetan Todorov (Paris: Editions du Seuil, 1981), 298.

24. Bakhtin, *Esthétique et théorie du roman*, 97.

25. Guy Scarpetta, "Sur plusieurs plans," *Art Press*, Hors Serie 4 (December 1984-February 1985), 40.

26. Jean-Luc Godard, *Introduction à une véritable histoire du cinéma*, tome 1 (Paris: Albatros, 1980), 66.

27. Louis Seguin, "Trouvé, certes, mais où?" *Positif* 93 (March, 1968), 41.

28. Bordwell, *Narration*, 322.

29. Robin Wood, "Godard and Weekend," *Weekend/Wind from the East* (London: Lorrimer Publishing, 1972), 12.

30. Jean-Luc Godard, "La Curiosité du sujet," interview by Dominique Paini and Guy Scarpetta, *Art Press*, Hors Serie 4 (December 1984-February 1985), 6.

31. Toby Mussman, "Duality, Repetition, Chance, the Unknown, Infinity," *Jean-Luc Godard*, ed. Toby Mussman (New York: E.P. Dutton, 1968), 301.

32. According to *La Nouvelle Biographie Générale*, tome 8 (Paris: Diderot Frères, 1855), Joseph Balsamo was a famous "imposter" living in Europe between1745 and 1795. He often pretended to be Count Alexander of Cagliostro, and Alexander Dumas later wrote about him in *Mémoires d'un médecine*.

33. Wood, 6.

34. Julia Kristeva, *Semiotika: Recherches pour une semanalyse* (Paris: Editions du Seuil, 1969), 241–42.

35. Marie-Claire Ropars-Wuilleumier, *De la Littérature au cinéma* (Paris: Librairie Armand Colin, 1970), 192.

36. Bordwell, *Narration*, 320.

37. Kristeva, *Semiotika*, 240.

38. Claude Greenberg, "Weekend," *Film et Vie* 39 (February-March 1968), 30.

39. Eco, *L'Oeuvre ouverte*, 62.

40. Scarpetta, 44.

41. Laurent Jenny, "The Strategy of Form," *French Literary Theory Today* (Cambridge: Cambridge Univ. Press, 1982), 44.

42. Eco, *L'Oeuvre ouverte*, 25.

43. Ibid., 59.

44. Waugh, 6.

45. Bakhtin, *Esthétique et théorie du roman*, 222.

46. Ibid., 227.

47. Godard, "La Curiosité du sujet," 5.

48. Godard, *Histoire*, 295.

49. Ibid., 253.

50. Scarpetta, 45.

51. Waugh, 6.

52. Bakhtin, *Esthétique et théorie du roman*, 213.

53. Waugh, 12.

54. Ibid., 81–82.

55. Sylvia Harvey, *May '68 and Film Culture* (London: BFI Publishing, 1980), 62.

56. Raymond Lefèvre, "Weekend," *La Revue du Cinéma* 308 bis (1976–77), 138.

57. Roland Barthes, *Le Plaisir du texte* (Paris: Editions du Seuil, 1973), 15.

58. Godard, *Histoire*, 295.

Chapter 6

1. Italo Calvino, *If on a Winter's Night a Traveler*, trans. William Weaver (New York: Harcourt Brace Jovanovich, 1979), 259.

2. Alexander Welsh, "Foreword," *Nineteenth Century Fiction* 33.1 (June 1978), 2.

3. Brooks, 314.

4. Mortimer, 212.

5. Edward Branigan, *Point of View in the Cinema* (New York: Mouton, 1984), 49.

6. Brooks, 52.

7. Francesco Casetti, "Looking for the Spectator," *Iris* 1.2 (4e trimestre, 1983), 22.

8. Jean-Pierre Oudart, "L'Idéologie moderniste dans quelques films récents: Un Discours en défaut," *Cahiers du Cinéma* 232 (September-October, 1971), 5.

9. Ibid., 7.

10. Welsh, 1.

11. Barthes, *Le Plaisir du texte*, 76.

Adam, Jean-Michel. *Linguistique et discours littéraire: Théorie et Pratique des textes.* Paris: Librairie Larousse, 1976.

Allen, Don. *Francois Truffaut.* London: Secker and Warburg Ltd., 1974.

Allen, Robert. *Speaking of Soap Operas.* Chapel Hill: Univ. of North Carolina Press, 1985.

Altman, Rick, ed. *Genre: The Musical.* Boston: Routledge & Kegan Paul, 1981.

Anderson, John R. *Cognitive Psychology and Its Implications.* New York: W. H. Freeman and Company, 1985.

Armes, Roy. *Patterns of Realism.* New York: A. S. Barnes and Company, 1971.

Aumont, Jacques, Alain Bergala, Michel Marie, and Marc Vernet. *L'Esthétique du film.* Paris: Editions Fernand Nathan, 1983. *Aesthetics of Film.* Translated and Revised by Richard Neupert. Austin: Univ. of Texas Press, 1992.

Aumont, Jacques. "Griffith, le cadre, la figure." *Le Cinema Americain.* Ed. Raymond Bellour. Paris: Flammarion, 1980. 51–67.

———. "Le Point de vue." *Communications* 38 (1983): 3–29.

———. "Points de vue: l'oeil, le film, l'image." *Iris* 1:2 (1983): 3–14.

Bakhtin, Mikhail. *Esthétique et théorie du roman.* Paris: Editions Gallimard, 1978.

———. *Le Marxisme et la philosophie du langage.* Paris: Editions de Minuit, 1977.

———. "La Structure de l'énoncé." *Mikhail Bakhtine le principe dialogique.* Ed. Tzvetan Todorov. Paris: Editions du Seuil, 1981: 287–316.

Bal, Mieke. "Narration et Focalisation: Pour une théorie des instances du récit." *Poétique* 29 (February 1977): 107–127.

———. *Narratologie: les instances du récit.* Paris: Klincksieck, 1977.

Barthes, Roland. "En Sortant du cinéma." *Communications* 23 (1975): 104–7.

———. *Image/Music/Text.* New York: Hill and Wang, 1977.

———. *Le Plaisir du texte.* Paris: Editions du Seuil, 1973.

———. "Le Problème de la signification au cinéma." *Revue Internationale de Filmologie* 32 (January–June 1960).

———. *S/Z.* Paris: Editions du Seuil, 1970. English Trans.: New York: Hill and Wang, 1974.

Bazin, André. *What is Cinema?* 2 vols. Berkeley: Univ. of California Press, 1971.

Beach, Joseph Warren. *The Twentieth Century Novel.* New York: Appleton-Crofts, 1932.

201

Bellour, Raymond. "Segmenting/ Analysing." *Genre: The Musical.* Ed. Rick Altman. Boston: Routledge and Kegan Paul, 1981.

———. "La Splendeur de soi-même." *Etudes Cinématographiques.* 28–29 (1963): 27–30.

Benveniste, Emile. *Problèmes de linguistique générale.* Paris: Gallimard, 1966.

———. *Problèmes de linguistique générale.* Vol. 2. Paris: Gallimard, 1974.

Bergala, Alain. "Initiation à la sémiologie du récit en images." Ligue Française de l'Ensign et de l'Education Permanente. Unpublished paper, 1984.

Bogdanovich, Peter. *John Ford.* London: Studio Vista, 1967.

Bondanella, Peter. *Italian Cinema: From Neorealism to the Present.* New York: Continuum, 1991.

Bordwell, David. "Art Cinema as a Mode of Film Practice." *Film Criticism* 4,1 (Fall 1979): 56–64.

———. "Happily Ever After, Part Two." *The Velvet Light Trap* 19 (1982): 2–7.

———. *Narration in the Fiction Film.* Madison: Univ. of Wisconsin Press, 1985.

———, Janet Staiger, and Kristin Thompson. *The Classical Hollywood Cinema: Film Style and Mode of Production to 1960.* New York: Columbia Univ. Press, 1985.

——— and Kristin Thompson. *Film Art.* New York: McGraw-Hill, 1993.

Branigan, Edward. *Point of View in the Cinema: A Theory of Narration and Subjectivity in Classical Film.* New York: Mouton Publishers, 1984.

Brémond, Claude. "La Logique des possibles narratifs." *Communications* 8 (1966): 60–76.

Bresson, Robert. *Notes sur le cinématographe.* Paris: Gallimard, 1975.

Brooks, Peter. *Reading for the Plot: Design and Intention in Narrative.* Cambridge: Harvard Univ. Press, 1992.

Browne, Nick. *The Rhetoric of Filmic Narration.* Ann Arbor: UMI Research Press, 1982.

Bruckner, Matilda Tomaryn. *Shaping Romance: Interpretation, Truth, and Closure in Twelfth Century French Fictions.* Univ. of Pennsylvania Press, 1993.

Brunette, Peter. *Roberto Rossellini.* New York: Oxford Univ. Press, 1987.

Bruss, Neal H. "The Transformation in Freud." *Semiotica* 17.1 (1976): 69–94.

Burch, Noel. *Theory of Film Practice.* Princeton: Princeton Univ. Press, 1981.

———. *To the Distant Observer.* Berkeley: Univ. of California Press, 1979.

Butor, Michel. *Inventory.* New York: Simon and Schuster, 1968.

Calvet, Louis-Jean. *Pour et contre Saussure: Vers une linguistique sociale.* Paris: Payot, 1975.

Calvino, Italo. *If on a Winter's Night a Traveler.* Trans. William Weaver. New York: Harcourt Brace Jovanovich, 1979.

Cannella, Mario. "Ideology and Aesthetic Hypotheses in the Criticism of Neo-Realism." *Screen* 14.4 (Winter 1973–74): 5–60.

Capdenac, Michel. "Weekend: L'Apocalypse selon Jean-Luc Godard." *Les Lettres Francaises* 1215 (January 3, 1968): 15.

Casetti, Francesco. "Looking for the Spectator." *Iris* 1, 2 (4e trimestre 1983): 15–30.

———. "Le Texte du film." *Théorie du film.* Ed. Jacques Aumont and Jean-Louis Leutrat. Paris: Editions Albatros, 1980. 41–65.

———. "Les Yeux dans les yeux." *Communications* 38 (1983): 78–97.

Charles, Michel. *Rhetorique de la lecture.* Paris: Editions du Seuil, 1977.

Chartier, J-P and F. Desplanques. *Derrière l'écran: Initiation au cinéma.* Paris: Editions SPES, 1950.

Chateau, Dominique. "Diégèse et énonciation." *Communications* 38 (1983): 121–54.

Chatman, Seymour. *Story and Discourse: Narrative Structure in Fiction and Film.* Ithaca: Cornell Univ. Press, 1978.

Colette, Jacques. "Discours narratif et jeu avec le temps." *La Narrativité.* Ed. Paul Ricoeur and Dorian Tiffeneau. Paris: Editions du Centre National de la Recherche Scientifique, 1980.

Collet, Jean and Jean-Paul Fargier. *Jean-Luc Godard*. Paris: Seghers, 1974.

Comolli, Jean-Luc and Jean Narboni. "Cinema / Ideology / Criticism." *Movies and Methods*. Ed. Bill Nichols. Berkeley: Univ. of California Press, 1976.

Coward, Rosalind and John Ellis. *Language and Materialism*. Boston: Routledge and Kegan Paul, 1977.

Creekmur, Corey K. "How Movies End: Narrative Closure in *Cruising*." *Purdue University Seventh Annual Conference on Film*. West Lafayette: Purdue Univ. Press, 1983: 140–44.

Croce, Arlene. "A Review." *Film Quarterly* 13.3 (Spring 1960): 35–38.

Culler, Jonathan. *On Deconstruction: Theory and Criticism after Structuralism*. Ithaca: Cornell Univ. Press, 1982.

———. *The Pursuit of Signs: Semiotics, Literature, Deconstruction*. Ithaca: Cornell Univ. Press, 1981.

———. *Structuralist Poetics*. Ithaca: Cornell Univ. Press, 1975.

Dallenbach, Lucien. *Le Récit speculaire: Essai sur la mise en abyme*. Paris: Editions du Seuil, 1977.

Denby, David, ed. *The 400 Blows*. New York: Grove Press, 1969.

Doane, Mary Ann. "Desire in *Sunrise*." *Film Reader 2* (January 1977): 71–77.

———. "The Dialogical Text: Filmic Irony and the Spectator." Diss. Univ. of Iowa, 1979.

Doniol-Valcroze, Jacques. "*Les Quatre cents coups*." *Cahiers du Cinéma* 96 (June 1959): 41–42.

Ducrot, Oswald, Tzvetan Todorov, Dan Sperber, Moustafa Safouan, Francois Wahl. *Qu'est-ce que le structuralisme?* Paris: Editions du Seuil, 1968.

Dufour, Fernand. "Un Exercice utile de Liberté." *Cinéma 68* 126 (May 1968): 94–97.

Eco, Umberto. *L'Oeuvre ouverte*. Paris: Editions du Seuil, 1965.

———. *A Theory of Semiotics*. Bloomington: Indiana Univ. Press, 1979.

Ellis, John. *Visible Fictions*. London: Routledge & Kegan Paul, 1982.

Fanne, Dominique. *L'Univers de Francois Truffaut*. Paris: Editions du Cerf, 1972.

Faye, Jean-Pierre. *Théorie du récit: Introduction aux langages totalitaires*. Paris: Collections Savoir Hermann, 1972.

Fehn, Ann, and Ingeborg Hoesterey, and Maria Tatar, eds. *Never Ending Stories: Toward a Critical Narratology*. Princeton: Princeton Univ. Press, 1992.

Fieschi, Jean-André. "The Difficulty of being Jean-Luc Godard." *Jean-Luc Godard*. Ed. Toby Mussman. New York: E. P. Dutton, 1968: 64–76.

Foucault, Michel. *L'Archéologie du savoir*. Paris: Editions Gallimard, 1969.

Gallagher, Tag. *John Ford: The Man and his Films*. Berkeley: Univ. of California Press, 1986.

Gardies, André. *Le Cinéma de Alain Robbe-Grillet: Essai sémiocritique*. Paris: Editions Albatros, 1983.

———. "Le Su et le vu." *Hors Cadre 2* (Spring 1984): 45–65.

Gardner, Howard. *The Mind's New Science: A History of the Cognitive Revolution*. New York: Basic Books, 1985.

Gaudreault, André. "Récit scriptural, récit théatrale, récit filmique: Prolégomènes à une théorie narratologique du cinéma." Diss. Paris: DERCAV Thèse de Doctorat de 3e Cycle, 1983.

Genette, Gérard. *Figures I*. Paris: Editions du Seuil, 1966.

———. *Figures II*. Paris: Editions du Seuil, 1969.

———. *Figures III*. Paris: Editions du Seuil, 1972.

———. "Frontières du récit." *Communications* 8 (1966): 152–63.

———. *Narrative Discourse: An Essay in Method*. Trans. Jane E. Lewin. Ithaca: Cornell Univ. Press, 1980.

———. *Nouveau discours du récit*. Paris: Editions du Seuil, 1983.

———. *Palimpsestes*. Paris: Editions du Seuil, 1982.

Gerlach, John. *Toward the End*. Birmingham: Univ. of Alabama Press, 1985.

Giles, Dennis. "Godard and Ideology." *Film Reader* 2 (January 1977): 169–79.

Gillain, Anne. *François Truffaut Le Secret perdu.* Paris: Hatier, 1991.

———. "The Script of Delinquency: François Truffaut's *Les 400 coups*." *French Film: Texts and Contexts.* Ed. Susan Hayward and Ginette Vincendeau. London: Routledge, 1990: 187–99.

Godard, Jean-Luc. *Cahiers du Cinéma* 138 (December 1962): 20–39.

———. "La Curiosité du sujet." Interview by Dominique Paini and Guy Scarpetta, *Art Press* Hors Serie 4 (December 1984–February 1985): 4–18.

———. *Le Gai savoir: mot à mot d'un film encore trop reviso.* Paris: Union des écrivains, 1969.

———. *Introduction à une véritable histoire du cinéma.* Paris: Editions Albatros, 1980.

———. "La Photo du mois." *Cahiers du Cinéma* 92 (February 1959): 44.

Gorbman, Claudia. *Unheard Melodies: Narrative Film Music.* Bloomington: Indiana Univ. Press, 1987.

Greenberg, Claude. "*Weekend.*" *Film et Vie* 39 (February–March 1968): 29–30.

Greimas, A. Julien. "Elements d'une grammaire narrative." *L'Homme* 9.3 (July–September 1969): 71–92.

Harvey, Sylvia. *May '68 and Film Culture.* London: British Film Institute, 1980.

Hayman, David and Eric S. Rabkin. *Form in Fiction.* New York: St. Martin's Press, 1974.

Heath, Stephen. *The Nouveau Roman: A Study in the Practice of Writing.* Philadelphia: Temple Univ. Press, 1972.

———. *Questions of Cinema.* Bloomington: Indiana Univ. Press, 1981.

Henderson, Brian. *A Critique of Film Theory.* New York: E. P. Dutton, 1980.

Houdebine, Jean-Louis. "Première approche de la notion de texte." *Théorie d'ensemble.* Paris: Editions du Seuil, 1968. 257–72.

Humphries, Reynold. *Fritz Lang cinéaste américain.* Paris: Editions Albatros, 1982.

Jefferson, Ann. *The Nouveau Roman and the Poetics of Fiction.* New York: Cambridge Univ. Press, 1980.

Jenny, Laurent. "The Strategy of Form." *French Literary Theory Today.* Cambridge: Cambridge Univ. Press, 1982.

Jost, François. "Les Aventures du lecteur." *Poétique* 29 (February 1977): 77–89.

———. "Discours cinématographique, narration: Deux facons d'envisager le problème de l'énonciation." *Théorie du film.* Ed. Jacques Aumont and Jean-Louis Leutrat. Paris: Editions Albatros, 1980. 121–31.

———. "Le Film: Récit ou récits?" *Cahiers du 20ᵉ Siècle* 9 (1978): 77–94.

———. "Narration(s): en deçà et au delà." *Communications* 38 (1983): 192–212.

———. "Pertinence narratologique et pertinence sémiologique." Unpublished paper, 1983.

———. "Vers de nouvelles approches méthodologiques." *Cinémas de la modernité.* Ed. D. Chateau, A. Gardies and F. Jost. Paris: Klincksieck, 1981.

Kayser, Wolfgang. "Qui raconte le roman?" *Poétique* 4 (1970): 498–510.

Kermode, Frank. *The Sense of an Ending.* New York: Oxford Univ. Press, 1967.

———. "Sensing Endings." *Nineteenth-Century Fiction.* 33.1 (June 1978): 144–158.

Kristeva, Julia, Jean-Claude Milner and Nicolas Ruwet. *Langue, discours, société: Pour Emile Benveniste.* Paris: Editions du Seuil, 1975.

Kristeva, Julia. *Le Texte du roman.* The Hague: Mouton, 1970.

———. *Semiotika: Recherches pour une sémanalyse.* Paris: Editions du Seuil, 1969.

Kuhn, Annette. *Women's Pictures: Feminism and Cinema.* Boston: Routledge and Kegan Paul, 1982.

Kuntzel, Thierry. "The Film-Work." *Enclitic* 2.1 (Spring 1973): 38–61.

———. "Le Travail du film, 2." *Communications* 23 (1975): 136–89.

Kuroda, S-Y. "Reflexions sur les fondements de la théorie de la narration." *Langue, discours, société.* Ed. Julia Kristeva, Jean-Claude Milner and Nicolas Ruwet. Paris: Editions du Seuil, 1975.

Lacan, Jacques. *Ecrits* I. Paris: Editions du Seuil, 1966.

Laffay, Albert. *Logique du cinéma: création et spectacle.* Paris: Masson, 1964.

———. "Le Récit, le monde et le cinéma." *Les Temps Modernes* 2.20/21 (April–June 1947): 1361–1375, 1579–1600.

Lang, Fritz. "Happily Ever After." *Penguin Film Review* 5 (1948): 22–29.

Laplanche, Jean and J. B. Pontalis. *Vocabulaire de la psychanalyse.* Paris: P.U.F., 1967.

Lefèvre, Raymond. "*Weekend.*" *Image et Son* 213 (February 1968): 117–21.

———. "*Weekend.*" *La Revue du Cinéma* 308bis (1976–1977): 134–39.

Leyda, Jay. *Kino.* New York: Collier, 1973.

Lotman, Iouri. *Semiotics of Cinema.* Trans. Mark E. Suino. Ann Arbor: Michigan Slavic Contributions, 1976.

———. *La Structure du texte artistique.* Paris: Gallimard, 1973.

MacArthur, Elizabeth J. *Extravagant Narratives: Closure and Dynamics in the Epistolary Form.* Princeton: Princeton Univ. Press, 1990.

MacBean, James Roy. "Godard's *Weekend,* or the Self-Critical Cinema of Cruelty." *Film Quarterly* 22.2 (Winter 1968–1969): 35–43.

MacCabe, Colin. "*Days of Hope*—A Response to Colin McArthur." *Screen* 17.1 (Spring 1976): 98–101.

———. *Godard: Images, Sounds, Politics.* Bloomington: Indiana Univ. Press, 1980.

Martin, Wallace. *Recent Theories of Narrative.* Ithaca: Cornell Univ. Press, 1986.

Metz, Christian. *Essais semiotiques.* Paris: Editions Klincksieck, 1972.

———. *Essais sur la signification au cinéma.* Vol. 2. Paris: Klincksieck, 1976.

———. *Film Language: A Semiotics of the Cinema.* New York: Oxford Univ. Press, 1978.

———. *Langage et cinéma.* Paris: Editions Albatros, 1977.

———. *Le Signifiant imaginaire.* Paris: Union Générale d'Editions 10/18, 1977.

Meyer, Leonard B. "The End of the Renaissance?" *Hudson Review* 16.2 (Summer 1963): 169–86.

———. *Music, the Arts and Ideas: Patterns and Predictions in Twentieth-Century Culture.* Chicago: Univ. of Chicago Press, 1967.

Millar, Gavin. "Claude Chabrol." *Cinema: A Critical Dictionary.* Ed. Richard Roud. London: Martin Secker & Warburg, 1980.

Miller, D. A. *Problems of Closure in the Traditional Novel.* Princeton: Princeton Univ. Press, 1981.

Miller, J. Hillis. "The Problematic of Ending in Narrative." *Nineteenth- Century Fiction.* 33.1 (June 1978): 3–7.

Monaco, James. *The New Wave.* New York: Oxford Univ. Press, 1976.

Morrisette, Bruce. *The Novels of Robbe-Grillet.* Ithaca: Cornell Univ. Press, 1971.

Mortimer, Armine Kotin. *La Clôture Narrative.* Paris: José Corti, 1985.

Mussman, Toby. "Duality, Repetition, Chance, the Unknown, Infinity." *Jean-Luc Godard.* Ed. Toby Mussman. New York: E. P. Dutton, 1968. 300–308.

Neale, Steve. "Art Cinema as Institution." *Screen* 22.1 (1981):11–40.

———. "New Hollywood Cinema." *Screen* 17.2 (Summer 1976): 117–22.

Neupert, Richard. "444,000 Images Speak for Themselves." *Wide Angle* 9.1: 50–58.

———. "*L'Immortelle*: The Ciné-roman and the Ciné-lecteur" *French Literature Series* 17 (1990) 35–41.

———. "The Musical Score as Closure Device." *Film Criticism* 14,1 (Fall 1989) 26–32.

Odin, Roger. "L'Entrée du spectateur dans la fiction." *Théorie du film.* Ed. J. Aumont and J. L. Leutrat. Paris: Editions Albatros, 1980.

———. "Modèle grammatical, modèles linguistiques et études du langage cinémato-graphique." *Cahiers du 20ᵉ Siècle* 9 (1978): 9–30.

Orr, Christopher. "Closure and Containment: Marylee Hadley in *Written on the Wind.*" *Imitations of Life: a reader on Film & Television Melodrama.* Ed. Marcia Landy. Detroit: Wayne State Univ. Press, 1991.

Oudart, Jean-Pierre. "L'Idéologie moderniste dans quelques films récents: Un Discours en defaut," *Cahiers du Cinéma* 232 (September–October, 1971): 4–12.

———. "Un Discours en défaut (2)," *Cahiers du Cinéma* 233 (November, 1971): 23–26.

Polan, Dana. "The Felicity of Ideology: Speech Acts and the 'Happy Ending' in American Films of the 1940's." *Iris* 3.1 (1985): 35–45.

———. *Power and Paranoia.* New York: Columbia, 1986.

Pottier, Bernard, ed. *Le Langage.* Paris: Centre d'Etude et de Promotion de la Lecture, 1973.

Prince, Gerald. "Introduction à l'etude du narrataire." *Poétique* 14 (1973): 179–96.

———. *Narratology: The Form and Functioning of Narrative.* New York: Mouton Publishers, 1982.

Recanati, Francois. *Les Enoncés performatifs.* Paris: Les Editions de Minuit, 1981.

Rhode, Eric. "A Review." *The 400 Blows.* Ed. David Denby. New York: Grove Press, 1969. 244–47.

Ricardou, Jean. *Le Nouveau roman.* Paris: Editions de Seuil, 1973.

Richter, David H. *Fable's End: Completeness and Closure in Rhetorical Fiction.* Chicago: Univ. of Chicago Press, 1974.

Ricoeur, Paul. *La Configuration dans le récit de fiction.* Paris: Editions du Seuil, 1984.

——— and Dorian Tiffeneau. *La Narrativité.* Paris: Editions du Centre National de la Recherche Scientifique, 1980.

Rimmon-Kenan, Shlomith. *Narrative Fiction: Contemporary Poetics.* New York: Methuen, 1983.

Rivette, Jacques. "Du Côté de chez Antoine." *Cahiers du Cinéma* 95 (May 1959): 37–39.

Robbe-Grillet, Alain. *Pour un nouveau roman.* Paris: Les Editions de Minuit, 1963.

Ropars-Wuilleumier, Marie-Claire. "Form and Substance, or the Avatars of the Narrative." *Focus on Godard.* Ed. Royal S. Brown. Englewood: Prentice-Hall, 1972.

———. "Fonction du montage dans la constitution du récit au cinéma." *Revue des Sciences Humaines* 141 (1971).

———. *De la Littérature au cinéma: Génèse d'une écriture.* Paris: Librairie Armand Colin, 1970.

———. *Le Texte divisé: Essai sur l'écriture filmique.* Paris: Presses Universitaires de France, 1981.

Rossellini, Roberto. "A Discussion of Neo-Realism." *Screen* 14,4 (Winter 1973–74): 69–78.

———. "Rossellini on Rossellini." *Screen* 14.4 (Winter 1973–74): 79–81.

Roud, Richard. *Godard.* Bloomington: Indiana Univ. Press, 1970.

Ruthrof, Horst. *The Reader's Construction of Narrative.* London: Routledge & Kegan Paul, 1981.

Sadoul, Georges. "The Importance of Subject Matter." *The 400 Blows.* Ed. David Denby. New York: Grove Press, 1969. 236–43.

Sahlins, Marshall. "Colors and Cultures." *Semiotica* 16: 1–22.

Saussure, Ferdinand de. *Cours de linguistique générale.* Paris: Payot, 1979.

Scarpetta, Guy. "Sur Plusieurs plans." *Art Press* Hors Serie 4 (December 1984–February 1985): 42–50.

Schatz, Thomas. *Hollywood Genres.* New York: Random House, 1981.

Schefer, Jean-Louis. *Scenographie d'un tableau.* Paris: Editions du Seuil, 1969.

Schnitzer, Luda and Jean. *Histoire du Cinéma Sovietique 1919–1940.* Paris: Pygmalion, 1979.

Seguin, Louis. "Trouvé, certes, mais où?" *Positif* 93 (March 1968).

Shklovsky, Victor. "La Construction de la nouvelle et du roman." *Théorie de la littérature.* Ed. Tzvetan Todorov. Paris: Editions du Seuil, 1965. 170–96.

Simon, Jean-Paul. "Enonciation et Narration." *Communications* 38 (1983): 155–91.

———. *Le Filmique et le comique: Essai sur le film comique.* Paris: Editions Albatros, 1979.

Smith, Barbara Herrnstein. *On the Margins of Discourse: The Relation of Literature to Language.* Chicago: Univ. of Chicago Press, 1978.

———. *Poetic Closure: A Study of How Poems End.* Chicago: Univ. of Chicago Press, 1968.

Staiger, Janet. *Interpreting Films.* Princeton: Princeton Univ. Press, 1992.

Sternberg, Meir. *Expostional Modes and Temporal Ordering in Fiction.* Baltimore: John Hopkins Univ. Press, 1978.

Sutton, Martin. "Patterns of Meaning in the Musical." *Genre: The Musical.* Ed. Rick Altman. Boston: Routledge and Kegan Paul, 1981. 190–96.

Thompson, Kristin. *Breaking the Glass Armor.* Princeton: Princeton Univ. Press, 1988.

———. "Sawing Through the Bough." *Wide Angle.* 1.3 (1976): 38–51.

Todorov, Tzvetan. "Les Catégories du récit littéraire." *Communications* 8 (1966): 125–51.

———. "Categories of the Literary Narrative." *Film Reader 2* (January 1977): 19–37.

———. *The Fantastic: A Structural Approach to a Literary Genre.* Ithaca: Cornell Univ. Press, 1975.

———. "La Lecture comme construction." *Poétique* 24 (1975): 417–25.

———. *Littérature et signification.* Paris: Librairie Larousse, 1967.

———. *Mikhail Bakhtine le principe dialogique.* Paris: Editions du Seuil, 1981.

———. *The Poetics of Prose.* Ithaca: Cornell Univ. Press, 1977.

———. *Poétique de la prose.* Paris: Editions du Seuil, 1971.

Tomasulo, Frank P. "The Rhetoric of Anti-Closure: Antonioni and the Open Ending." *Purdue University Seventh Annual Conference on Film.* West Lafayette: Purdue Univ. Press, 1983. 133–39.

Torgovnick, Marianna. *Closure in the Novel.* Princeton: Princeton Univ. Press, 1981.

Truffaut, François. *The Adventures of Antoine Doinel.* Trans. Helen Scott. New York: Simon and Schuster, 1971.

———. *Correspondence: 1945–1984.* Ed. Gilles Jacob and Claude Givray. Trans. Gilbert Adair. New York: Noonday Press, 1989.

———. *Les Films de ma vie.* Paris: Editions du Cerf, 1972.

Turim, Maureen. *Flashbacks in Film: Memory and History.* New York: Routledge, 1989.

Ubersfeld, Anne. *L'Ecole du spectateur.* Paris: Editions Sociales, 1981.

Vanoye, Francis. *Récit écrit-récit filmique.* Paris: Editions CEDIC, 1979.

Vernet, Marc. *Figures de l'absence.* Paris: Cahiers du Cinéma, 1988.

Waller, Gregory A. "See it Through: Closure in Four Horror Films." *Purdue University Seventh Annual Conference on Film.* West Lafayette: Purdue Univ. Press, 1983. 17–24.

Walsh, Martin. "Godard and Me: Jean-Pierre Gorin Talks." *The Brechtian Aspect of Radical Cinema* London: BFI, 1981. 116–28.

Watson, George. *The Story of the Novel.* London: MacMillan Press, 1979.

Waugh, Patricia. *Metafiction.* London: Methuen, 1984.

"*Weekend.*" *Le Film Francais* 1225 (5 January 1968): 2.

Welsh, Alexander. "Foreword." *Nineteenth-Century Fiction* 33.1 (June 1978):1–3.

Wexman, Virginia Wright. *Creating the Couple: Love, Marriage, and Hollywood Performance.* Princeton: Princeton Univ. Press, 1993.

Williams, Christopher. "Bazin on Neo-Realism." *Screen* 14.4 (Winter 1973–1974): 61–68.

Wollen, Peter. *Readings and Writings: Semiotic Counter-Strategies.* London: Verso Editions, 1982.

Wood, Robin and Michael Wallace. *Claude Chabrol.* New York: Praeger, 1970.

Wood, Robin. "Godard and *Weekend.*" *Weekend/Wind from the East.* London: Lorrimer, 1972.

Zazzo, René. "Espace, mouvement et Cinemascope." *La Revue Internationale de Filmologie.* 5.18–19 (July–December 1954): 209–19.

Index

209